PRAISE FOR
The 9 to 5 Window

In his book *The 9 to 5 Window*, Os Hillman equates work with worship and shows this to be a deeply spiritual truth. By following his guidance, we can all make the secular sacred and thus transform our lives. Don't miss this splendid book!

Ken Blanchard

COAUTHOR, *THE ONE MINUTE MANAGER®* AND *THE SECRET*

It has been my experience that the marketplace ministry movement is having a significant impact on the Kingdom, and Christians are realizing that God has equipped and called them to their present location as their field of ministry. I am delighted that Os Hillman, who has been working with marketplace leaders for many years, has written this book, *The 9 to 5 Window*. I recommend it to those who are serious about integrating their faith into their work environment.

Ron Blue

CHRISTIAN FINANCIAL PROFESSIONALS NETWORK
ATLANTA, GEORGIA

As a former businessman, I'm delighted to see the growing movement of "marketplace ministries" encouraging Christians to serve God where they spend most of their time—on the job. Not only does *The 9 to 5 Window* address issues that have caused believers to separate work and ministry, but it also provides a host of guiding principles to those who want to effectively impact their workplaces for Christ. This book helps all of us to see ourselves as ministers!

Dr. Tom Fortson

PRESIDENT AND CHIEF EXECUTIVE OFFICER, PROMISE KEEPERS

The Savior didn't just call us to a life *inside* the Church but also to a life that is *outside* of it, and He's calling each of us to honor Him in all that we say, think and do—especially on the job. *The 9 to 5 Window* is a practical, insightful and thought-provoking book. Not only will its message transform your workplace, but it will also transform your life. Os Hillman is a true vessel of God, complete with briefcase and a Bible!

Andria Hall
FORMER NEWS ANCHOR, CNN
AUTHOR, *THE WALK AT WORK: SEVEN STEPS TO SPIRITUAL SUCCESS ON THE JOB*

Os Hillman gives us a comprehensive coverage and update on the workplace ministry movement, revealing that it is growing tremendously and spreading throughout the world. In this book you will find all the attributes, principles and miraculous works that God is using to cause His Kingdom to come and to be manifested beyond the walls of the local church. Every Christian needs to read this book and incorporate its truths concerning saints manifesting the kingdom of God in the marketplace.

Dr. Bill Hamon
CHAIRMAN, CHRISTIAN INTERNATIONAL BUSINESS NETWORK
BISHOP, CHRISTIAN INTERNATIONAL APOSTOLIC NETWORK
AUTHOR, *DAY OF THE SAINTS*

Jesus Christ is moving in the workplace today in so many unique ways. Os Hillman shows us how to join God in this 9 to 5 window of opportunity. Travel with Os on this journey and marvel at the variety of ways the Spirit of God is empowering ordinary believers to transform their workplaces for Christ.

Kent Humphreys
PRESIDENT, FELLOWSHIP OF COMPANIES FOR CHRIST INTERNATIONAL
OKLAHOMA CITY, OKLAHOMA

If your faith life and your work life are important to you, you will not want to miss *The 9 to 5 Window*. It provides practical answers on how to live out your faith radically yet practically. Os has given us a book of depth and substance for those who want to be instruments of transformation in work and life.

Laurie Beth Jones
FOUNDER, THE JONES GROUP
AUTHOR, *JESUS, CEO; THE PATH* AND *JESUS IN BLUE JEANS*

When Os Hillman started talking about the 9 to 5 window, I knew he had put the whole marketplace movement into perspective. The workplace needs to be impacted for the Lord, and this book tells us how to do it. I loved the book, and I am confident that you will too.

Rich Marshall
AUTHOR, *GOD@WORK* AND *GOD@WORK VOLUME 2*
FOUNDER, ROI LEADERSHIP INTERNATIONAL

Os Hillman is a man uniquely gifted to both describe and help shape what God is doing in the marketplace ministry movement. His insights in this book, *The 9 to 5 Window*, confirm this.

Dennis Peacocke
PRESIDENT, STRATEGIC CHRISTIAN SERVICES

The 9 to 5 Window is an exciting, practical and challenging read for every Christian businessperson. Os brings across the challenges facing all of us in the marketplace, with many great examples and solutions. It is my prayer that this great book will inspire millions to lead and run their business on Kingdom principles.

Graham Power
PRESIDENT, POWER GROUP OF COMPANIES
VISIONARY, TRANSFORMATION AFRICA AND GLOBAL DAY OF PRAYER

Os Hillman has written a book that is extremely practical and genuinely profound. Os addresses how to resolve the tension between the pulpit and the marketplace by showing pastors what is in the heart of Christians who feel a call to ministry but not to the pulpit. He draws on his own insights but also on what he constantly gleans from others in his God-given networking ministry. This book is a superb how-to manual and a must-read for all Christians.

Ed Silvoso

PRESIDENT, HARVEST EVANGELISM, INC.
AUTHOR, *ANOINTED FOR BUSINESS*

Arguably, Os Hillman is the most knowledgeable person today in the rapidly escalating Faith at Work movement. *The 9 to 5 Window* will give you an accurate, thorough and enjoyable overview of one of the most crucial things that the Spirit is saying to the churches in this season.

C. Peter Wagner

PRESIDING APOSTLE, INTERNATIONAL COALITION OF APOSTLES
PRESIDENT, GLOBAL HARVEST MINISTRIES
CHANCELLOR, WAGNER LEADERSHIP INSTITUTE

Os Hillman has long been a leader in the Faith at Work movement, and many of our students, staff and alumni at Regent University have been inspired by his work. Os now continues his leadership with this incisive, important book, helping Christians to reframe their work from God's perspective.

Michael Zigarelli

DEAN, REGENT UNIVERSITY SCHOOL OF BUSINESS

9 THE to 5 window

OS HILLMAN

Regal

From Gospel Light
Ventura, California, U.S.A.

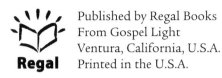

Published by Regal Books
From Gospel Light
Ventura, California, U.S.A.
Printed in the U.S.A.

Regal Books is a ministry of Gospel Light, a Christian publisher dedicated to serving the local church. We believe God's vision for Gospel Light is to provide church leaders with biblical, user-friendly materials that will help them evangelize, disciple and minister to children, youth and families.

It is our prayer that this Regal book will help you discover biblical truth for your own life and help you meet the needs of others. May God richly bless you.

For a free catalog of resources from Regal Books/Gospel Light, please call your Christian supplier or contact us at 1-800-4-GOSPEL *or* www.regalbooks.com.

Cover Illustration, Ed Tuttle, Eklektos, www.eklektosdesign.com

Any omission of credits is unintentional. The publisher requests documentation for future printings.

Library of Congress Cataloging-in-Publication Data
Hillman, Os.
  The 9 to 5 window / Os Hillman.
     p. cm.
  Includes bibliographical references.
  ISBN 0-8307-3796-0 (hardcover), 0-8307-3849-5 (trade paperback)
  1. Work–Religious aspects–Christianity. 2. Vocation. I. Title: Nine to five window. II. Title.
  BT738.5.H55 2005
  248.8'8–dc22   2005011545

1   2   3   4   5   6   7   8   9   10   /   10   09   08   07   06   05

Rights for publishing this book in other languages are contracted by Gospel Light Worldwide, the international nonprofit ministry of Gospel Light. Gospel Light Worldwide also provides publishing and technical assistance to international publishers dedicated to producing Sunday School and Vacation Bible School curricula and books in the languages of the world. For additional information, visit www.gospellightworldwide.org; write to Gospel Light Worldwide, P.O. Box 3875, Ventura, CA 93006; or send an e-mail to info@gospellightworldwide.org.

DEDICATION

This book is dedicated to my friends, colaborers and advisory board members of the International Coalition of Workplace Ministries (ICWM), who have been a source of encouragement and an example of what it means to live a life of faith in the 9 to 5 window.

Angie Hillman, ICWM/Marketplace Leaders, Atlanta, GA

Andria Hall, SpeakEasy M.E.D.I.A., Scotch Plains, NJ

Brenda deCharmoy, Consultant, South Africa

Colin Ferreira, International Christian Chamber of Commerce, Port of Spain, Trinidad

Dennis Doyle, Nehemiah Partners, Minneapolis, MN

Denton Cormany, Priority Associates, Raleigh, NC

Dennis Peacocke, Strategic Christian Services, Santa Rosa, CA

Doug Spada, His Church at Work, Atlanta, GA

Jan Christie, Voices of Prayer/ICWM, Cleveland, GA

Johnny and Elizabeth Enlow, Daystar Church, Altanta, GA

Kent Humphreys, Fellowship of Companies for Christ, Oklahoma City, OK

See-Lok Ting, Center for Marketplace Leadership, Malaysia

Mike McLoughlin, YWAM Marketplace Missions, Kelowna, British Columbia, Canada

Tim Habeck, The Covenant Group, Atlanta, GA

CONTENTS

ACKNOWLEDGEMENTS

Writing a book requires lots of input and multiple rewrites and revisions before the final version is complete. It is a process that requires the skills of many others once the initial manuscript is complete.

I want to thank my soul mate and wife, Angie, for her considerable time, feedback and personal editing skills she provided as we got to the point of giving the manuscript to Regal Books. She has been a trusted friend, wife and editor for much of my work. She is a great sounding board and spiritual companion with me in this journey.

Once we moved into the editing process there were several others who made major contributions to this work, including Kathy Deering, Deena Davis and Mark Weising with the Regal Books team.

I particularly want to thank Bill Greig III for his faith in this work and the vision he is showing by making an investment in this very important category.

God bless you all!

INTRODUCTION

We are convinced that England will never be converted until
the laity use the opportunities daily afforded by their various
professions, crafts and occupations.
Towards the Conversion of England (1945)

What happens when Christian believers take the Word of God literally and
begin to apply it where they spend 60 to 70 percent of their waking hours?

What happens when they use their spiritual authority in their work
lives, reflecting their spiritual value system in their area of influence?

What happens when Christians move in a spiritual dimension in
their work lives as few have endeavored to do before now?

What happens is that lives, workplaces, cities and nations begin to be
transformed by the power of Christ. Jesus' prayer in Matthew 6:10, "Thy
kingdom come . . . Thy will be done on earth, as it is in heaven" (*KJV*),
becomes a reality in the here and now.

In the first Reformation, Martin Luther did us a great service by
bringing the *Word* of God to the common man and woman. The second
Reformation is taking the *work* of God to the common man and woman.
We are now seeing early glimpses of what can happen in and through the
life of a Christian who is willing to break the sacred/secular divide that
has held sway since the days before the Reformation.

However, we have yet to be fully liberated. At present, it is reported
that less than two percent of the population attends church in England.
It has become a secularized society because the above warning issued in
Towards the Conversion of England in 1945 was not heeded by the Christian
leaders of the day. America is rapidly moving in the same direction if
something does not change.

For years, the organized Church has sought to make an impact on the
culture through various religious activities, such as city prayer meetings,
pastor unity meetings, spiritual warfare conferences, intercessory prayer,
spiritual mapping, and so on. These activities are very important, yet we

have not seen one major city transformed for Jesus Christ. Why is that?

It is because we in the Church have not equipped or commissioned those who have the authority in the cities to impact their spheres of influence for Jesus Christ. We have not helped them to realize that they *are the army of the Lord*—not merely the supporting personnel who supply the tools and equipment to those in the Church.

We have wrongly equated "ministry" to what takes place inside the four walls of the local church. We have failed to affirm the worker at IBM, the clerk at Wal-Mart, the nurse at the hospital or the sixth-grade teacher at the elementary school that the work they do five days a week is as important as any ministry they do within the four walls of their local congregation. In fact, surveys reveal that more than 90 percent of church members do not feel they are being equipped by the Church to apply their biblical faith in their daily work life. As a result, they are ineffective for Christ at their places of employment, which allows the culture to continue to take away spiritual ground from the kingdom of God. In other words, by not equipping those in the Church to impact their workplaces for Christ, we give over every area of society to the kingdom of darkness.

In the pages that follow, you will discover what it takes to experience God's power in your day-to-day working life. I am convinced that most of us have never experienced God's presence in our work because we have not understood what is required of us to receive it. We have lived so much on *principles* that we have missed the way to live in His *presence* as it relates to our vocational calling.

You will also learn new biblical truths that apply to your daily work life. You will read incredible stories about the new breed of worker who has gone beyond the status quo to become a transformer in his or her sphere of influence. You will discover why I believe there is a God-birthed movement now underway that could become a societal "tipping point."

I invite you to walk with me as we enter new territories still unclaimed for the kingdom of God. However, beware. You may never be the same after our journey.

—Os Hillman

PART I:

UNDERSTANDING YOUR CALL

CHAPTER 1

SATAN'S DECEPTIONS ABOUT YOUR WORK

*Therefore, my brothers, be all the more eager to make your calling
and election sure. For if you do these things, you will never fall, and you
will receive a rich welcome into the eternal kingdom of our
Lord and Savior Jesus Christ.*

2 PETER 1:10-11

I first met John Wigington in 1999 when he attended one of my first Called to the Workplace workshops in Atlanta. John is a classic example of a man who loves God and has been called to the marketplace since his early teens. However, after graduating from high school, John assumed that his only option for serving God was in full time vocational ministry. He believed that his passion for Christ meant he was to become a pastor or a missionary. His pastor even encouraged this idea. This can be one of Satan's greatest deceptions. Here is John's story in his own words:

> Since childhood, I had loved God with all my heart. I loved to
> read and study my Bible, along with many of the great Christian

classics, but I also enjoyed books about business and economics. In the seventh grade, I became very interested in the stock market. In high school, I began reading the *Wall Street Journal* and many other business magazines.

The summer after I graduated high school was a special time in my walk with the Lord. I read many books about discipleship and memorized large portions of Scripture. Before starting my freshman year of college, I went to my pastor and told him all that God was doing in my life, and that I wanted to give my life and future to Him. I dreamed of writing for the *Wall Street Journal* or *Forbes* magazine. I could see myself becoming a stockbroker or investment banker.

But that was not what my pastor saw. He said that he believed God was calling me into the ministry to become a preacher. So I spent three years in a Bible college, when I should have spent four years in a business school learning to apply my business skills through a Kingdom perspective to transform Wall Street for Jesus Christ.

Shortly after graduating from Bible school, John decided to pursue a career in financial management, and today he is a stockbroker on Hilton Head Island in South Carolina. However, for years John struggled with guilt for being in business after going to Bible School. It was not until he attended one of my workshops that he began to see things differently. As John states,

Before I attended your Called to the Workplace workshop, I felt that the enemy had put a false sense of guilt upon me for being in business. This rendered me ineffective both in my walk with the Lord and in my business. I couldn't understand what God was doing. It wasn't until the workshop that I understood and saw what the Lord had been doing and preparing me for since childhood. For the first time, I realized I wasn't called to vocational ministry—I was *already in ministry!* I was called to be a follower of Christ and my destiny was business.

There are many stories like John's out there. I hear them almost weekly. Satan has deceived many workplace believers about seeing their vocations in a spiritual manner. Here are a few of his lies:

- Our jobs are not spiritual—they are useful only to make money for the church.
- Our vocations have no spiritual authority.
- Our secular employment is not to be mixed with the church's ministry activities.
- "Ministry" is what takes place within the four walls of the church building.

Furthermore, there seems to be an unspoken spiritual hierarchy that ranks vocations based on the level of a person's spirituality and commitment to serve God. My friend Mark Greene from the London Institute of Contemporary Christianity describes the ranking this way:

1. Pastor (absolute highest spiritual vocation)
2. Overseas missionary
3. Evangelist
4. Paid church worker
5. Vocational parachurch ministry worker
6. Housewife
7. Plumber
8. Advertising agency executive (lowest of the low . . . down there with "lawyer")

Mark and I both came out of the advertising business so we can poke fun at our former professions as advertising agency executives. The Scriptures are clear that there is no vocation less spiritual than any other if it is done with honesty, integrity and a heart to serve God. "Whatever you do, work at it with all your heart, as working for the Lord, not for men, since you know that you will receive an inheritance from the Lord as a reward. It is the Lord Christ you are serving" (Col. 3:23-24). In regard to spiritual value, whether you are called to be a plumber, a doctor, a secretary or a CEO, your calling is equal to that of the pastor or vocational Christian worker. The key is to be in the place where God has called you and to live for the glory of God in that place.

God Uses Our Work

How does God call people into His service? As we read through the Scriptures, we find that many have been called while they were in the midst of performing their everyday vocation. Peter was a fisherman, Matthew was a tax collector, Luke was a physician, Paul was a tentmaker, Jesus was a carpenter, and so on.

Moses was a shepherd who was going about his normal workday when God called him to His Service. Since killing an Egyptian man 40 years earlier when he saw him beating one of his Hebrew brethren, Moses had been living out his days as a shepherd—a very lowly profession in the eyes of an Egyptian. He was now 80 years old, and the last thing on his mind was a new adventure. He was ready to collect his pension, his past life only a faded memory. Although deep inside he might have felt he was destined for something greater, the event 40 years earlier reminded him of a good impulse that went extremely bad.

So, Moses was minding his own business, tending sheep on the far side of the desert, when he noticed that a bush was on fire. Even more startling, it was not burning up! Then, alarmingly, a voice came from the bush—which I guess should be no surprise since he was standing on Mount Horeb, the mountain of God. If God were going to speak, this would be a good place.

The voice belonged to God. God told Moses in great detail about the huge rescue mission He wanted him to lead to free the Israelites from Egypt. Moses was not at all interested in this proposition and he argued with God about the whole idea. Among other things, I am sure that he remembered he was a wanted man in Egypt. In the midst of his protests, God asked Moses a simple question: "What is that in your hand?" (Exod. 4:2).

Moses was holding his shepherd's staff. *What can that have to do with anything?* he must have thought. God went on to explain, "Take *this staff* in your hand so you can perform miraculous signs with it" (Exod. 4:17, emphasis added).

A few years ago, while attending a conference, I heard a message about the significance of the staff in the life of the Hebrew. The speaker had met a pastor who had just returned from Israel and who had brought back a replica of the type of staff a Hebrew would have owned in biblical times. He had learned that a staff was more than a shepherd's tool. When the shepherd made his staff, he added a creosote-type substance to the wood to insure its hardness so that it would last a lifetime. Typically, he marked his staff up and down to represent significant dates and events that had happened in his life. It was like a personal diary, if you will.

The fact that God wanted to use Moses' *staff* to perform miracles is significant because the staff represented not only Moses' work, but it also, most importantly, represented his life. The staff was a symbol of Moses' calling in life as a shepherd. It was the identifying tool of his vocation. God was saying, in essence, "I am going to take your vocation and perform miracles through it." He wanted Moses to look at his work in a new and powerful way.

When God called Gideon to free the people of Israel from the oppression of the Amalekites, He did so while Gideon was on the job threshing wheat. Like Moses, Gideon argued with God; he also felt he was too insignificant to be used by God to save Israel. Nevertheless, Gideon acknowledged God by preparing an offering to Him. An angel of the Lord did an interesting thing with the offering: "With the tip of the staff that was in his hand, the angel of the Lord touched the meat and the unleavened bread. Fire flared from the rock, consuming the meat and the bread. And the angel of the Lord disappeared" (Judg. 6:21).

As with Moses, God had chosen to do a miracle with Gideon's staff, the instrument that symbolized his work and his life. What is God trying to show us by doing this? He wants us to know that our work and our lives are the tools He wants to use to demonstrate His power. However, in order for that to happen, we must yield them to Him.

The Deceptions of the Enemy

There is an identity crisis taking place today among Christians in the workplace. Satan desires to render Christians useless in their workplace calling, and his strategy is to make them feel that their work is meaningless or that it is a curse. The following are some of the deceptions Satan uses to accomplish this strategy.

Deception #1: Work Is Meaningless

A San Francisco radio station survey reveled that an incredible 80 percent of respondents said that they were dissatisfied with their work. A survey conducted by the *Wall Street Journal* found that 50 percent of executives were dissatisfied with their work. The study also confirmed that 80 percent of people among the general workplace population were dissatisfied with their work. Additionally, a survey of 500 Christians taken by Doug Sherman and Bill Hendricks, authors of *Your Work Matters to God,* revealed an alarming 50 percent dissatisfaction rate.[1]

What does this tell us? It tells us that most people are finding little meaning and purpose in their work lives, even Christians. Today's workers lack purpose in their work life as never before. It is of crisis proportions. Believers have not been taught the spiritual value of their work.

Deception #2: Work Is Cursed

"Cursed is the *ground* because of you; through painful toil you will eat of it all the days of your life. *It will produce thorns and thistles for you,* and you will eat the plants of the field. By the sweat of your brow you will eat your food until you return to the ground, since from it you were taken; for dust you are and to dust you will return" (Gen. 3:17-19, emphasis added).

The importance of work was first established in Genesis when God put Adam in the Garden of Eden "to work it and take care of it" (Gen. 2:15b). God entrusted the garden to Adam and Eve's care and gave them authority over it. But when they sinned against Him, their relationship changed. No longer would their work be a blessing. From then on, it was going to be hard, because the ground was cursed and more difficult to cultivate.

Today, many Christians believe their work is a curse. This is not a biblical truth. It was the *ground* that was cursed, which made work more difficult. My friend Ed Silvoso observes that he doesn't believe it was by accident that the Romans placed a crown of thorns on Jesus' head before they nailed Him to the cross. Could it be that those thorns represented more than just an additional source of pain? Could it be that they represented the fallen world described in Genesis 3:18 that would "produce thorns and thistles"?

Biblical Truths Regarding Work

In the film *The Passion of the Christ*, produced by Mel Gibson, there is a wonderful scene that shows Jesus working as a carpenter. It is my favorite scene in the movie, and it gives us a rare glimpse of what His everyday life might have been like before His public ministry began.

Admittedly, God's strategy for sending the Savior of the world seems a little odd. Jesus was born into a working-class family. He worked with His father Joseph in his carpentry business until age 30, so most of His adult life was given to "secular" labor. To build His Church, He chose 12 men who came straight from the workplace and who had no religious credentials for ministry.

Jesus' ministry focused on the marketplace, where people spent most of their time. Of His 132 public appearances in the New Testament, all but 10 of them were in the marketplace, and 45 of His 52 parables had a workplace context. It is also interesting to note that of the 40 divine encounters and miracles listed in the book of Acts, 39 occurred in the workplace.

Truth #1: Jesus Redeemed Work

Not only did Christ identify and minister to those in the workplace, He also redeemed work. Jesus' death on the cross restored those things that were lost in the Fall. "For the Son of Man has come to seek and to save *that* which was lost" (Luke 19:10, *NASB*, emphasis added). Notice that the Scripture says He saved *that* which was lost, not *who* was lost. What was lost in the Garden of Eden? It was man's relationship with God—his innocence and his ability to work the ground without sweat and toil. No longer would work be the joy it was intended to be. However, when Jesus died, He became the source of restoration for all that was lost in the Garden. Paul reinforces this in Colossians 1:19-20: "For God was pleased to have all his fullness dwell in him, and through him to reconcile to himself *all things*, whether things on earth or things in heaven, by making peace through his blood, shed on the cross" (emphasis added).

Yes, He restored *all* things—including the relationship between mankind and his work. No longer should we labor out of sweat and toil, for God has restored the joy to our labor that He intended in the first place. In fact, one form of the word "work" comes from the Hebrew word *avodah,* which means worship.

Jesus' desire was for God's kingdom to be manifested on Earth. When He taught the disciples to pray, He petitioned His heavenly Father by asking, "Your kingdom come, your will be done on earth as it is in heaven" (Matt. 6:10). While we may never see God's kingdom completely evidenced on Earth as it is heaven, Jesus *is* telling us that we should ask for it and expect it.

Once we understand that Jesus died to redeem our work and that it's possible to see His kingdom here on Earth, we are on our way to understanding another key point—God has need of our work to accomplish His purposes.

Truth #2: Our Work Has a Purpose

"Now when they drew near Jerusalem, and came to Bethphage, at the Mount of Olives, then Jesus sent two disciples, saying to them, 'Go into the village opposite you, and immediately you will find a donkey tied, and a colt with her. Loose them and bring them to me. And if anyone says anything to you, you shall say, "The Lord has need of them," and immediately he will send them'" (Matt. 21:1-3, *NKJV*).

The donkey was a symbol of commerce in Jesus' day. Donkeys provided a source of income to people by trampling seed, turning millstones to grind grain and pulling plows. Donkey caravans were the freight trains and transport trucks of ancient times. These animals could carry great weight despite their small size, and since they required only a fraction as much fodder as a horse, they were more economical to own.

When Jesus told the disciples to go untie the donkey, He was taking over someone's work and source of income. The disciples no doubt felt a bit uneasy about fulfilling His request, but Jesus had need of that donkey to make His triumphal entry into Jerusalem during His last week of ministry.

Legend has it that God etched a cross onto the back of a donkey's neck to symbolize the role it would play in the life of Jesus. As it turns out, this legend is true. An owner of a donkey ranch in Texas explains, "All donkeys have a cross mark on their back, with the vertical part extending from the neckline down the backbone and the horizontal extending left and right across the front shoulders. The mark is very prominent on grey donkeys but isn't visible in the hair on white or black donkeys. However, if you shave them to the skin, the mark can be seen."

Jesus had need of the donkey in His day. He has need of our "donkeys" today. Let me explain.

The night before I was to speak at a workplace conference in Singapore, the Lord prompted me to read the passage in Matthew 21:1-3 regarding the donkey. I sensed He wanted me to relay the message that just as He needed the donkey in His day, He needed the people of Singapore to give Him their "donkeys" because He has need of them to accomplish His purposes today. Even though I felt uncomfortable about including such an unusual concept in my message, I added it to my PowerPoint presentation.

The next morning, I went down for breakfast and was joined by Maggie, an intercessor from Malaysia. I knew Maggie well. She had prepared for this conference by fasting and praying for 40 days, and I asked her if the Lord had spoken to her about this conference during her prayer time. "Oh, yes," she said. "He told me on September 21 that the Singapore business people were to give their 'donkeys' to Him." I smiled.

That afternoon, I asked the attendees to come forward and give their "donkeys" to the Lord for His use to build His Kingdom here on Earth through the workplace. More than 200 people came forward.

A New Beginning

God has called each of us into our vocations. He wants to bring His presence into our vocations so that He can demonstrate His power in them. However, many of us have held on to our donkeys. They are still tied to the tree of sin and sweat and toil. Our work has become the beast of burden in our lives.

Satan wants to deceive you into thinking that the only reason you work is to earn a living. He wants you to think your work life is not a calling. He wants you to live only for the material things in life. But Jesus came to redeem our lives and our livelihoods for His purposes. He can give us rest in the midst of our work lives so that our work is not burdensome. Our workplaces can become centers of freedom, joy and worship.

God is calling forth believers today to see their vocations as instruments of transformation. Until now, most of us have seen our work as a mere instrument for earning income. God is changing this paradigm. Our work represents much more. It is an instrument designed to transform our lives and workplace (and, by extension, our cities and nations) into places of freedom and love. Why does God want to demonstrate His power through us in this way? "So that they may believe that the Lord, the God of their fathers—the God of Abraham, the God of Isaac and the God of Jacob—has appeared to you" (Exod. 4:5).

God desires to reveal His glory through every person on Earth. We spend most of our waking hours at work. Whether you're a housewife, an educator, a businessman, a student, or in the military, God desires to live His life and make His presence known in the 9 to 5 window. He wants to perform miracles through your "staff."

Are you willing to let Him use yours?

How About You?

1. Have you fallen for Satan's deception that God has no interest in your work?
2. Are you willing to turn your vocation over to the Lord? Why not pray a prayer of commitment to the Lord and ask Him to use your work life for His glory?

CHAPTER 2

UNDERSTANDING YOUR PURPOSE

*For we are God's workmanship, created in Christ Jesus to do good works,
which God prepared in advance for us to do.*

EPHESIANS 2:10

If you are going to discover how God wants to use your life and work, you must know why you were created. If you start trying to determine your purpose in life before understanding why you were created, you will inevitably get hung up on the *things you do* as the basis for fulfillment in your life, which will only lead to frustration and disappointment.

First and foremost, God created you to know Him and to have an intimate relationship with Him. In fact, God says that if a man is going to boast about anything in life, "boast about this: that he understands and knows me" (Jer. 9:24). Mankind's relationship with God was lost in the Garden when Adam and Eve sinned. Jesus' death on the cross, however, allows us to restore this relationship with God and to have an intimate fellowship with Him. The apostle Paul came to understand this when he said, "I gave up all that inferior stuff so I could know Christ personally, experience his resurrection power, be a partner in his suffering, and go all the way with him to death itself" (Phil. 3:10, *THE MESSAGE*).

Establishing this relationship with God is vital to understanding your purpose. If you don't have this relationship with God, you will seek to fulfill your purpose out of wrong motives, such as fear, insecurity, pride, money, relationships, guilt or unresolved anger. God's desire is for you to be motivated out of love for Him and to desire to worship Him in all that you do. As you develop your relationship with God, He will begin to reveal His purpose for your life. "'For I know the plans I have for you,' declares the Lord" (Jer. 29:11).

Your purpose in life is chosen by God. It is not negotiable. It is like calling water wet—there is no changing that fact, and there's no changing God's purpose for your life. While you may not *fulfill* the purpose for which you were made, you still *have a purpose* that God intends for you to fulfill. This is your blueprint from God. In the same way that He had a specific purpose in mind for Jesus when He sent Him to the earth, He has a specific purpose in mind for your life.

This doesn't mean, however, that there is one highly specific niche for you to fill and that if you miss it, too bad. It is my belief that you can achieve your purpose in many different and creative ways. This should take the pressure off. You won't throw your entire life off course by choosing the wrong college, job or mate. God is much bigger than any miscalculation or disobedience on your part. "The Lord will fulfill his purpose for me" (Ps. 138:8). Isn't that comforting to know?

Defining your purpose will help you to determine the activities that you should be involved in. Like Jesus, you should not involve yourself in activities that contradict His purpose for your existence. Jesus' purpose was to do the will of the Father, and He never did anything contrary to that purpose. In the same way, your purpose should always be to do the will of the Father.

Several years ago, Henry Blackaby wrote a popular Bible study, *Experiencing God: Knowing and Doing His Will*, in which he described how one of the core principles is to join God where He is already working in order to find His purpose for your life. When you involve yourself in activities contrary to this purpose, you

- begin to live a life of sweat and toil that leads to slavery instead of reaching the Promised Land of His rest
- get off course from achieving the intended destiny for your life
- produce dead works instead of the fruit of obedience rooted in your purpose
- potentially lose your reward because you are involved in activity God never orchestrated.

Each of us must ask *why* we are involved in an activity. Is it a God-activity, or just a good activity? Remember, Jesus only did something if He saw the Father doing it—and He was able to see what His Father was doing because of His intimate relationship with Him.

Discovering My Purpose

I discovered my purpose late in life. I grew up thinking that my destiny was to be the next Jack Nicklaus.

I started playing golf when I was 11 years old, and my dad encouraged me greatly in this area. I eventually became a very good junior player and even received a golf scholarship to the University of South Carolina. I thought I was well on my way to becoming a professional golfer on the PGA Tour; but when I finished school and turned pro, I quickly grew frustrated and disillusioned with my inability to get to a level to play competitively as a professional.

Our family had always been a church-going family, but we knew little of the concept of walking in a personal relationship with God. However, when I was 14, my dad was killed in an airplane crash, and this accident ultimately led my mom to a more intimate relationship with God. Through her influence and that of a pastor, I became a Christian in 1974.

As the years went by, I decided that golf was no longer the profession I felt God wanted me to be in. I made a career change into sales and marketing, but after being in various jobs for six years, I found myself longing to grow more in the Lord and serve Him in a greater capacity. I was involved in starting a church with two other men who were seeking to be used by God, and this led me to begin thinking about whether I was really "sold out" for God and needed to go to seminary. "Perhaps I am really called to be a pastor," I thought to myself. I decided to take a leave of absence from my job and go to a three-month Bible study course. I then decided to move to Atlanta to serve as an assistant pastor, only to have the position removed after three months. This caused me to go back into the business world. In hindsight, I see that this was the hand of God.

Through it all, I learned that I was never cut out to be a pastor or to have a "vocational ministry"; I was designed to be in business. On the other hand, I could not help but think of myself as a "second-class" Christian who was not quite sold out to the purposes of God. I don't believe that anyone was saying this to me; it was more implied by the Christian culture around me.

In 2002, I met a woman named Brenda who specialized in working with executives in career transition. She had a keen understanding of how to help people understand their core purpose in life from God's perspective, and she challenged me to go through this process. The goal at the end of the day was to create a five- to seven-word statement that defined my God-given purpose. It took an entire day of tiresome exercises, but in the end we came up with this statement: The purpose for which God made Os Hillman is to *articulate and shepherd foundational ideas for transformation.*

During this process we identified many core strengths that I have, such as teaching, networking, communicating and writing. All of these were attributes of my life, but the core purpose was to articulate and shepherd foundational ideas that could lead to transformation. The interesting thing is that my core purpose had been modeled as a teaching golf professional, a business consultant and an advertising agency owner. I had "articulated and shepherded" ideas in these arenas. Today God is doing it in a spiritual way through writing, mentoring and leading a movement to help people understand their work as a calling.

Understanding Your Anointing

In addition to understanding your purpose, you also need to understand the anointing that is on your life. We read about God's anointing in Scripture: "As for you, the anointing you received from him remains in you, and you do not need anyone to teach you. But as his anointing teaches you about all things and as that anointing is real, not counterfeit—just as it has taught you, remain in him" (1 John 2:27).

Anointing is a gift that functions easily when it is operating in you to the benefit of others and the kingdom of God. In his book *Anointing: Yesterday, Today and Tomorrow*, R. T. Kendall explains it this way:

> The best way I have been able to describe [an anointing] is that it is when our gift functions easily. It comes with ease. It seems natural. No *working it up* is needed. It is either there or it isn't. If one has to work it up one has probably gone outside one's anointing. If one goes outside one's anointing the result is often fatigue—that is, weariness or spiritual lethargy that has been described as "dying inside."[1]

One area in which I have a God-given anointing is networking. I have never sought to develop such an anointing, but I sure know a *lot* of people. Despite being an introvert, God has connected me with people all around the world. Many times people call me about something and my natural response is, "Oh, you need to contact so-and-so. He can help you with that."

My wife, Angie, has an anointing in the area of disarming people. She "unstuffs" people faster than anyone I know. There is no way that you can be a stuffy person around Angie. She is no respecter of persons, either. One of our good friends, a dignified lawyer from Nigeria, does not smile a lot and is quite serious most of the time. As we were leaving a conference one time, Angie noticed him having a serious meeting with three other men in the nearby restaurant. She ran over and gave him a great big, demonstrative kiss on the cheek to say goodbye. He was flabbergasted and did not know what to do. Later he smiled at Angie and said, "Angie, you are something else!" I have seen people open up to Angie when they will not open up to anyone else. It is her anointing. Everyone is her best friend after a short time.

Where do you move naturally in your life? What do you do that you don't have to work at? Chances are, that is your anointing. God wants you to walk in the anointing He has given to you for His glory.

Being Promoted Beyond Your Anointing

Understanding your anointing will also enable you to know when you are moving in a direction away from that which God has intended for your life. R. T. Kendall explains how many believers often find themselves lured into accepting promotions and assignments outside of their anointing—a concept known as the "Peter Principle":

> The way the Peter Principle works is this. A person who has been a first-rate typist or secretary may find themselves in management. As long as they were typing letters, taking dictation, or answering the telephone they were superb. They coped with ease. But a vacancy at a higher level came along and they applied for and got the job. They now have to make hard decisions, handle people under them, and find that they are under stress. They are not cut out for this after all—but try to stick it out. The have been promoted to the level at which they are not able to function with ease. They should have stayed with their old job. But no. They are determined to make it work. Few people will admit they have been promoted to the level of their incompetence.[2]

I have seen this principle happen a lot over the years. In my ministry, I have some key intercessors who support me personally. One time, I made the decision to put one of these individuals into the role of coordinating prayer for an event because she was an awesome intercessor who had a keen ability to hear God. However, I soon discovered that she was a poor networker and organizer. I had placed her in a role in which her anointing did not lay. That was a good lesson for me.

My Weakness, His Strength

There is a paradox between these two concepts that cannot be ignored. Sometimes, God will place you in situations in which you have no natural gifting. In these cases, God puts you there to experience His power in order to accomplish your tasks. Again, my wife, Angie, is a good example of this. Before she came to work with me full-time, she was a marketing and advertising manager for a non-profit organization. This organization hired a career consulting company to take all their employees through a series of tests to determine if each employee fit into his or her proper job function.

When the results of Angie's test were shared with the rest of her team, her profile revealed that one of her greatest weaknesses was lack of organization and focus. Her boss took exception to the assessment and publicly acknowledged that Angie was the most detailed and organized individual on the entire team. "How could that be true?" he asked.

The consultant said, "Oh, I am glad you asked that. Angie is a perfect example of someone who has overcome her weakness, because even though she recognizes this is her natural bent, she has overcome this by learning to be focused and detailed." In essence, she had yielded this area to the Holy Spirit and God had worked through her weakness.

I have seen this in my life as well. I am not a natural public speaker. I am generally a shy and reserved person. In a group of people, I will usually be the one to speak the least. But when you give me a topic that I am passionate about, such as helping people find God's calling for their lives, I will talk your head off. I was never one to speak in public, but because the message is more important than my comfort level, God began to empower me to speak publicly about the message He had placed in my heart.

God often moves us beyond our natural gifting and allows us to receive things through our obedience to Him. Oswald Chambers provides some valuable insight on this when he states, "The call of God only becomes clear as we obey, never as we weigh the pros and cons and try to reason it out. The call is God's idea, not our idea; and only on looking back over the path of obedience do we realize what God's idea has been all along."[3]

Often, God has to get us in a position to accept a call from Him. For many of us, this requires some sort of motivation for us to seek God. More often than not, this motivation comes through some calamity or crisis. When a crisis takes place in our lives, we begin to seek God for relief and answers. Over time, this process encourages us to seek God's face (in a personal relationship) instead of merely His hand of provision.

I believe most of us will experience many jobs and experiences on our way to discovering the purpose or destiny for which God made us. For some of us, that destiny will not be an event or a specific thing, but a process over our lifetime. However, although you may have a similar experience to mine, you also may be someone who starts out in the right place for your calling. The apostle Paul makes an interesting statement that indicates that most of us will remain in the very jobs in which we came to know the Lord. He writes, "Usually a person should keep on with the work he was doing when God called him" (1 Cor. 7:20, *TLB*). God has uniquely gifted you to perform a work in and through the workplace. And in most cases, He wants you to remain in that place to fulfill His purposes through your workplace calling.

How About You?

God has made you for a purpose. When you begin to walk in that purpose, you will have a better understanding of what activities should be in your life and how to make better decisions.

1. Why do you believe God made you? List five attributes of your life that make you, *you*.
2. What might hinder you from fulfilling God's purpose? (Our website, www.faithandworkresources.com, has tools to help you discover your purpose. See the section, "Your Calling.")

CHAPTER 3

FINDING YOUR PURPOSE

I will give you the treasures of darkness, riches stored in secret places, so that you may know that I am the Lord, the God of Israel, who summons you by name.

ISAIAH 45:3

Many times, the way God calls us into His purpose for our work life is through a hardship of some kind. In other words, He "breaks" our staff, or our vocation. The purpose of the breaking is not to destroy us, but to bring us to a place of willingness to lay down our vocations so that God can use them. The breaking prepares our heart for the new calling.

In Exodus 4, God required Moses to lay down his staff in order for him to see it as something that had power. As soon as Moses obeyed, God changed his staff into a snake. Notice what one commentary says about this act of obedience:

> The turning of Moses' staff into a serpent, which became a staff again when Moses took it by the tail, had reference to the calling of Moses. The staff in his hand was his shepherd's crook, and

represented his calling as a shepherd. At the bidding of God, he threw it upon the ground, and the staff became a serpent, before which Moses fled. The giving up of his shepherd-life would expose him to dangers, from which he would desire to escape. At the same time, there was more implied in the figure of a serpent than danger, which merely threatened his life. The serpent had been the constant enemy of the seed of the woman (Gen. 3), and represented the power of the wicked one, which prevailed in Egypt. But at the bidding of God, Moses seized the serpent by the tail, and received his staff again as "the rod of God," with which he smote Egypt with great plagues. From this sign the people of Israel would necessarily perceive that Jehovah had not only called Moses to be the leader of Israel, but had endowed him with the power to overcome the serpent-like cunning and the might of Egypt; in other words, they would believe that Jehovah, the God of the fathers, had appeared to him.[1]

God was instructing Moses to lay down that which represented his life and calling, so that He could transform it and raise it up for His purposes. Once Moses laid his staff down and then took it back up, a significant change took place. It was no longer only his shepherd's staff; it was the "staff of God." "So Moses took his wife and sons, put them on a donkey and started back to Egypt. And he took the *staff of God* in his hand" (Exod. 4:20, emphasis added).

God's staff has power. After Moses' staff became God's, it was used as the instrument of deliverance and transformation for the people of God. It delivered people out of the slavery of Egypt through one of the most dramatic miracles of all time—the parting of the Red Sea (see Exod. 14:16). Moses' staff transformed a people from slavery to freedom and was used to demonstrate his God-given authority.

Circumstantial Setbacks

Saul was trying to solve a problem in his dad's business when God called him to be king of Israel. We read in 1 Samuel 9—10 about how Saul was working for his father, Kish, in the family business. We don't know what type of business it was, but it required the use of donkeys. As we discussed in chapter 1, donkeys transported goods and were the key commercial distribution system of the day. Kish had lost some of his donkeys. No doubt, his distribution system was severely affected. So he asked his son Saul to find them.

Saul took a servant with him and they spent the day searching unsuccessfully in four different places. It was getting late and he was ready to abandon the search. At the end of his resources, Saul was now in the perfect position for God's divine intervention. Like Saul, most of us attempt to solve our problems as well as we can, and often we are not in a position to hear God's answer to our problem until we have exhausted all of the options in our own strength.

Just when Saul was ready to quit searching, his servant spoke up and said, "Look, in this town there is a man of God; he is highly respected, and everything he says comes true. Let's go there now. Perhaps he will tell us what way to take" (1 Sam. 9:6). Saul decided to take his servant's advice, and two began to look for the prophet.

On the way, they met two young girls who told them where and when the man of God would be in the city. (God often uses situations that seem very incidental in pointing us to the way He has for us.) Following the girls' directions, they ran right into the prophet Samuel. Immediately, Samuel told Saul that his father's donkeys had been found, but that there was more to this meeting than that. He anointed Saul with oil and told him that God had chosen him to be king over Israel. He specifically described signs and wonders that were about to take place in his life. What must Saul have thought? All he intended to do was to find his dad's donkeys and suddenly he found himself talking to a prophet who said he was going to be king.

In his book *Experiencing God: Knowing and Doing His Will,* Henry Blackaby writes, "You cannot go with God and stay where you are."[2] God must change us if we are going to fulfill His purposes in our lives. Samuel said to Saul, "The Spirit of the Lord will come upon you in power, and you will prophesy with them; and you will be changed into a different person" (1 Sam. 10:6). Up to this point, Saul had never prophesied or led a group of people. He had also never had to be accountable to a prophet and to God for his every action.

Saul took a big step of faith right away and prophesied with the prophets just as Samuel said he would. How exciting that must have been. Yet, when Samuel called the entire nation of Israel together to announce him as Israel's first king in history, Saul was nowhere to be found. This part of the story is humorous. Excitement is in the air, but when they call Saul's name, he doesn't even come forward. So the people "inquired further of the Lord, 'Has the man come here yet?' And the Lord said, 'Yes, he has hidden himself among the baggage'" (1 Sam. 10:22).

For us, this should be an encouragement. God continues to pick the foolish things of this world to confound the wise. Your greatest setback can be thinking that there's no way that God can use "little me." However, the reality is that He can and will, if we respond properly to the negative circumstances around us.

The Joseph Calling

Joseph had a tremendous calling on his life that ultimately resulted in his becoming a physical and spiritual provider over nations. However, God had to do extensive breaking and preparation in his life to make him ready.

By 1994, I had a life that many people would have longed for. I had made enough money to retire at the age of 44; I was playing golf about three times a week, and my walk with God was "adequate" in my eyes— or at least not much different from any other Christian businessperson I knew. Then one day, my wife of 14 years announced that she wanted to separate. This led to a divorce three years later. At the same time, investments of more than $500,000 disintegrated over a period of a few months, and I lost 80 percent of my business along with clients who failed to pay bills that added up to more than $140,000. My world quickly changed from having a successful small business and family to having no family, little money and a shell of a business. My world had fallen apart, and I was devastated.

I had heard stories of other business people who had gone through difficult times and had always looked at them with a judgmental attitude, thinking they probably had made unwise choices and were reaping from those choices. My problems, though, did not stem from unwise choices. At least they didn't appear that way to me. I was forced to find answers.

So, for the next two years, I sought answers. I questioned what I had done wrong and why God had allowed this to happen to me. During the first year, a man came into my life who helped me to work on control issues related to my character. The next year another man came into my life who provided insights into what God was trying to accomplish in my life. Finally, two years into the process, someone sent me an audio-tape from a Swedish businessman named Gunnar Olson, the founder of the International Christian Chamber of Commerce (ICCC).

In that tape, Gunnar talked about a phenomenon that he called the "Joseph Process." He described how many people go through great trials in their business life as part of a calling by God to be a "Joseph" in their day. This piqued my interest a great deal, and when I learned Gunnar Olson was going to be in Washington, D. C., the next month to host the ICCC international conference, I knew that I needed to go and meet him.

I flew to Washington, D.C., and was able to arrange a meeting with Gunnar at his hotel. When I walked into his suite, Gunnar asked me to tell my story, and for the next few minutes I recounted my narrative in every gory detail. When I finished, he looked at his fellow board member, James Lockett, and began to chuckle.

I couldn't believe his response. At that moment, I did not know whether to stand up and leave or smack the guy. However, Gunnar immediately apologized and said, "We are not trying to be rude to you. We have heard this story so often that it is simply uncanny to us. Be assured, my friend, you are one of God's Josephs He has called." From that moment, my life began to take on a whole new perspective.

Learning about the Joseph Process was the first glimmer of hope in what I had viewed as a hopeless situation. It was as if a heavy weight had been lifted from my shoulders, and for the first time I saw my circumstances in a new light. I no longer saw the reason for my problems as something I had done to myself. Sure, I had not been perfect in my life, but the kinds of problems I was experiencing were much larger than the mistakes that I may have made.

Spiritual Boot Camp

In Exodus 2, we read how Moses had been on the backside of the desert for 40 years because he had tried to do God's work in his own way. Moses had known back then that there was a call upon his life, and after he had murdered the Egyptian, "Moses thought that his own people would realize that God was using him to rescue them, but they did not" (Acts 7:25). His God-given desire to free his people was mixed with his human methods of achievement—manipulation, violence and force. And because God never calls us to fulfill His plan in our own strength, He had to lay Moses aside for 40 years in order to "remove the Egypt" from his life.

In Scripture, Egypt always represents a place of slavery, sweat, toil and manipulation. And there is no better way to remove the Egypt from our lives than to remove us totally from the old system that taught us. There had to be a season of separation to change Moses' paradigm. In the desert, he entered a new season of learning and usefulness in the hand of God. His failure was now going to be an instrument of wisdom to build something new in his life and in the life of a nation.

Moses' 40 years in the desert was a process of maturation that was required for him to become God's man. The Bible says that Moses was the most humble man on the face of the earth (see Num. 12:3). Humility, obedience and faith are the traits God requires of those He uses in a significant way. Moses didn't have all of these traits when he began. It required a divine encounter and then a process. God does the same with each of us.

Just as Moses had to spend 40 years in the desert before he could fulfill God's call on his life, Joseph also had to go through a spiritual "boot camp." Joseph's spiritual boot camp was 13 years long and required a separation from his former life. It involved a breaking of his will and his ability to control anything. He was forced to choose to believe that God was still in control of the events in his life.

My friend Bob Mumford once said, "Beware of any Christian leader who does not walk with a limp." It is often this kind of preparation that is needed to get the man or woman ready for God's use. Like Jesus, Joseph suffered for those he would ultimately save. He was rejected by his own people. He provided spiritually for those he was called to serve. God invested a lot in Joseph for this special calling—a calling that would save an entire nation and the world from starvation. At the age of 30, Joseph was one of the youngest rulers in history, and God could not afford to have a man in this position with any pride. Joseph's years of trials and testing were designed to remove any vestiges of pride in his life and to build an unshakable relationship with God.

Four Tests

God took Joseph through four unique tests. I believe that Joseph was required to pass each one successfully before he qualified for the next. When he passed the last one, he was finally elevated for the call that God ultimately had on his life.

Test #1: Loving Your Enemies

Joseph's first test involved his family's rejection. His brothers had sold him to slave traders. What could be worse than to have your own family sell you into slavery? It would be very easy to fall into bitterness toward your family and God if something like this happened to you. Betrayal is one of the most difficult tests in life, and it often comes from one's own family or those in the Body of Christ. Every day, you and I must work and live in environments that do not treat us in an honorable manner. Sometimes, it's downright cruel.

I believe some of these experiences are actually allowed in our path in order to find out how we are going to handle them. A. W. Tozer said, "It is doubtful whether God can bless a man greatly until he has hurt him deeply."[3] Most leaders who are used mightily by God have experienced a Judas-type of betrayal at one time or another. Whether or not God later elevated them was dependent upon how they handled the situation.

I believe our response to betrayal is God's graduate-level course in our walk with Him. King David had a similar test when his closest companions created a source of pain in his life. We read of his struggle in Psalm 55:12-14, where he states, "If an enemy were insulting me, I could endure it; if a foe were raising himself against me, I could hide from him. But it is you, a man like myself, my companion, my close friend, with whom I once enjoyed sweet fellowship as we walked with the throng at the house of God." Bitterness and unforgiveness have disqualified many people from moving on in the kingdom of God. God will not elevate you if there is any root of bitterness in your life. If you have something against a brother or sister, you must forgive him or her if you expect God to bless your life.

I had a very close friend who had become a mentor to me. We were the best of friends. However, an issue arose in our relationship that turned out to be very negative. It was very painful, but God used the situation to show me exactly how Jesus must have felt when Judas, one of his closest companions, betrayed him. I decided to bless this man in very tangible ways even though he refused to resolve our differences. Five years later, he asked to reconcile our relationship. I believe that this would not have happened if I had not taken the initiative to "love my enemy." Are you willing to wash the feet of Judas, as Jesus did?

Test #2: Moral Purity

The second test for Joseph was in the area of moral purity. Joseph was living in Pharaoh's palace and he had not been around women for a long time. To make matters worse, his boss's wife began to make passes toward him, which can be a huge temptation for any man. However, Joseph did the only thing anyone can do to withstand sexual temptation—he fled. He passed the purity test.

Judah, however, did not. In Genesis 38, we read how Judah, one of the 12 sons of Jacob, allowed his purity—and his very staff—to be taken from him. Judah had just lost his wife, and after mourning her death he went on a little trip to Timnah. His widowed daughter-in-law, Tamar, posed as a prostitute, and Judah succumbed to sexual temptation, having intercourse with his dead son's wife. The form of payment was supposed to be a young goat, but because Judah didn't have one with him at the time, Tamar asked for a pledge.

> "Will you give me something as a pledge until you send it?" she asked.
> He said, "What pledge should I give you?"
> "Your seal and its cord, and *the staff* in your hand," she answered. So he gave them to her and slept with her, and she became pregnant by him (Gen. 38:17-18, emphasis added).

Judah gave up his staff—the one thing that represented his very life and work—to a woman who would later frame him with it. Sexual failure is like this. It requires everything from you. When you encounter sexual temptation, you must be like Joseph and flee. You cannot overcome sexual temptation any other way.

Men, especially, need to take heed and stay away from compromising situations. You do not want to be disqualified because of failure in this area. Even your computer can be a source of sexual temptation.

Test #3: Perseverance

The third test for Joseph was perseverance. Joseph had been in prison for many years. He had successfully interpreted a dream for some powerful people who could deliver him from prison. It is clear that Joseph had his hopes up, but he was not released. He remained in prison for another two years. Joseph was tired of being in prison, but there was something inside that kept him going. He persevered.

This is one of the most difficult aspects of the Joseph process, for it can take many years to get through this stage. Scripture tells us, "hope deferred makes the heart sick" (Prov. 13:12). Many will give up the fight at this point, and they may even consider taking their own lives. When my advertising agency was successful, I had a staff of seven people. When my world fell apart, I was by myself for five years—alone and forced to do the best I could to satisfy creditors and make ends meet. At times, it seemed like a never-ending treadmill. But God was doing a deeper work than I could see at the time. He was building character. He was removing pride.

He was preparing me for something hand-tailored for me.

The test of perseverance is the one that many people cannot endure. All too often, they will move when God tells them to be still and wait. They will decide that they have been waiting long enough, so they set out to deliver themselves. This is a big mistake. If God has not completed the deeper work, He will take you around the mountain one more time—or even more if that is what is necessary to complete the inner work that He has begun in your life.

The depth and width of your calling is often proportional to the depth of the faith experiences in your life that come through adversity. A faith experience is any encounter you have with God that allows you to experience Him in a greater dimension. God frames your life through these experiences in order to speak to others. Moses' Red Sea miracle was a faith experience. Joshua's crossing the Jordan was a faith experience. However, if we short-circuit God's process in our lives by delivering ourselves out of our difficult circumstances, we will miss some incredible faith experiences. Perseverance is of vital importance if we are to enter God's promised land for our lives.

Test #4: Stewardship
After 13 years of slavery and imprisonment, Joseph was finally freed from prison and elevated to the second highest position in Egypt. I wonder what that must have been like. Joseph performed well in his new role. He was a good steward. He passed the most challenging test of all—stewardship over prosperity.

When God began to change my difficult circumstances (after seven years), the funny thing was that it just didn't make that much difference anymore. I had learned to live in that difficult state and had become satisfied that I could live in it forever if I had to. In essence, I had finally "died." In Romans 6:4, Paul instructs us that we must die in order for Christ to be resurrected in each of our lives.

How can you tell when your adversity will be over? I believe your adversity will be over when it doesn't matter anymore. When Joseph was elevated to his high position, he was able to do it without fanfare, because he had learned to be content in his hard circumstances.

Four years into my Joseph Process, I began attending a new church. Now divorced and wondering what life would be like as a single 44-year-old Christian man, a woman sat next to me in church. She was pretty. She was single. To my surprise, God allowed a friendship to develop. Nine months later, I was married to Angie. And seven years after the start of my crisis, God allowed me to sell a piece of property that allowed me to pay off all of my debts and become debt-free. He had delivered me.

A Modern Joseph

My friend, Louisiana businessman Bill Hamm, went through his Joseph Process in 1999. Bill liked his life the way it was. He was a tithing church-goer who was doing well in his work. Then the contracting business in which he held a 50 percent stake lost seven million dollars. The next three years were the most stressful of his life. He went into severe depression. He ended up selling off the division that had lost all the money and spent a million dollars on legal fees for three major litigations against his company.

The experience brought Bill to the end of himself, and he learned to be totally dependent on God to meet all his needs. He recalls, "I used those years to 'sow in tears' as the psalmist exhorts us to do. Like Joseph, God made me fruitful in the land of my suffering."

During that time, God gave Bill a vision for bringing the Kingdom into the marketplace and a passion for helping people see their work as a calling and a ministry. To fulfill the vision, God led Bill in an unusual way. He had been introduced to the idea that God can give creative concepts to people—"witty inventions." A friend told him about an invention that had potential in the oil business. Through a series of developments that enabled him to invest time and money in the new technology, Bill was able to bring it to a worldwide market.

However, it was not back to business as usual. Bill set up a team of 18 intercessors to establish a prayer foundation for the business. They prayed for a year and a half before they had the formation documents in place. Bill is convinced that without this prayer foundation, the company would have failed. As they transitioned into the implementation phase, this group of intercessors became a spiritual board of directors that continued to pray for the day-to-day business matters.

The five startup partners see their business as a ministry and a conduit for blessings to flow into the Kingdom. Although the oil company promises to generate massive returns, they believe the primary focus is how the Lord wants to use their company and the technology of which they have been made stewards. Bill's Joseph Process prepared him for his new venture.

Stewards of His Resources

As God's Josephs, we go through trials so that we can be fully yielded to His purposes. God has His way of taking us aside to get our undivided attention. For Paul, it was Arabia for three years; for Moses, it was 40 years in the desert; for Joseph, it was 13 years in Egypt.

God knows the stubborn human heart. He knows that if He is to accomplish His deepest work, He must take us into the desert in order to give us the privilege of being used in His Kingdom. In the desert, God changes us and removes things that hinder us. He forces us to draw deep upon His grace. If He had not allowed me to be plunged into a desert season in my own life, I would not have known what He was calling me to do. Even my unusual name, Os, turned out to be significant to the process.

I am a third generation business owner. My real name is Omar Smallwood Hillman III. Quite a mouthful. My parents put the "O" and the "S" together to call me Os. No one in my family knows where the name "Omar" came from. We only know that "Smallwood" was the name of the doctor who delivered my grandfather.

During my desert season, one of my mentors challenged me to find out more about the meaning of my name. He felt it was important for me to know as I tried to figure out God's call for my life. He also wondered if my father had been distracted or deflected from pursuing a similar call, leaving me to pick up the reins.

Throughout the Bible, we find that names were given as an indication of God's purpose for an individual. In some cases, names were altered to represent a significant change, as in Abram to Abraham, Saul to Paul, Jacob to Israel, or Sarai to Sarah. When I looked up the name "Omar," I discovered that it was Arabic for "first son" and "disciple," Hebrew for "gifted speaker" and German for "famous." In the Bible, Omar was a grandson of Esau (see Gen. 36:15), and another meaning of his name means "eloquent." Esau, as you will remember, had forfeited his birthright for a bowl of pottage.

What gave significance to this series of meanings was that both my father and my grandfather may have become distracted from God's calling for their lives, based upon the limited history I could piece together. It appeared that God was giving me a chance to fulfill this call. It was like putting a puzzle together, especially in light of the recent events in my own business career.

I was the first and only son of my parents. . . . I am a disciple of Jesus Christ. . . . I felt that God was calling me to public speaking. The puzzle pieces were beginning to come together.

Apparently, my Joseph Process included becoming a steward of God's resources for God's people in the workplace. Part of my job would be to help other descendents of Esau *recover their birthrights,* even though they may have sold their birthright for earthly pleasure and prestige or remained in Egypt as brick-makers instead of moving to the Promised Land. To make sure that I was an instrument fully yielded to His purposes, God had to break my vocation decisively, sending me into oblivion for a time, before He could bring me out and use me.

Someone once said, "God uses enlarged trials to produce enlarged saints so He can put them in enlarged places!"[4] The desert is only a season in your life. When God has accomplished what He wants, He will bring you out. He has given you a mission to fulfill that can only be fulfilled after you have spent an adequate time of preparation in the desert. Don't fear the desert, for it is there that you will hear God's voice as never before. It is there that you will have the idols of your life removed. It is there that you will begin to experience the reality of a living God as never before.

How About You?

1. Recount the four tests Joseph endured. Is there anyone in your life from whom you need to seek forgiveness? Make a decision to extend grace to that person.

2. What are some things God has taught you through adversity? Thank God today for what you have learned through your adversity.

FOUR ATTRIBUTES OF AN EFFECTIVE WORKPLACE WITNESS

May the favor of the Lord our God rest upon us; establish the work of our hands for us—yes, establish the work of our hands.

PSALM 90:17

If I were to ask you to describe the core attributes of a person who exemplifies God's ideal for a Christian in the workplace, what would you say? This is the most common question I get from the secular media.

Over the past several years, I have observed four key qualities exhibited by workplace believers who are transforming their workplaces for Christ. I believe these attributes are God's ideal for the Spirit-led worker today. Let's take a look at them.

Attribute #1: A Quality of Excellence

Several years ago, I published a magazine devoted to Christians in the workplace. When I gave a copy to a friend, he looked at it and said, "This doesn't even look like a *Christian* magazine." What did he mean? He was saying the quality of many products that Christians produce tend to be less than the quality of non-Christian products—which is an indictment on the work of Christians.

One of the four ways we can make an impact for Christ on our workplace is by doing our work with excellence. In the Bible, Bezalel was a man handpicked by God to perform an important work—to design and build the Ark of the Covenant. He was also the first man described in Scripture as being filled with the Spirit of God: "Then the Lord said to Moses, 'See, I have chosen Bezalel son of Uri, the son of Hur, of the tribe of Judah, and I have filled him with the Spirit of God, with skill, ability and knowledge in all kinds of crafts—to make artistic designs for work in gold, silver and bronze, to cut and set stones, to work in wood, and to engage in all kinds of craftsmanship'" (Exod. 31:1-6). The work of Christians should be excellent in every way because we have the Spirit of God operating in us.

Daniel and his friends were also exceptional in their work. "The king talked with them, and he found none equal to Daniel, Hananiah, Mishael and Azariah; so they entered the king's service. In every matter of wisdom and understanding about which the king questioned them, he found them ten times better than all the magicians and enchanters in his whole kingdom" (Dan. 1:19-20). Later, the Scriptures make a point of the fact that Daniel was favored by his employer because of the exceptional job he did. "It pleased Darius to appoint 120 satraps to rule throughout the kingdom, with three administrators over them, one of whom was Daniel. Now Daniel so distinguished himself among the administrators and the satraps by his exceptional qualities that the king planned to set him over the whole kingdom" (Dan. 6:1-3). Daniel was the model civic worker. He did his job well, which was why his boss respected him.

Atlanta-based Chick-fil-A, Inc. is the country's second-largest quick service chicken restaurant chain. The company's stated corporate purpose is "to glorify God by being a faithful steward of all that is entrusted to us, and to have a positive influence on all who come in contact with Chick-fil-A." The company is a great example of a business that is modeling religious principles and producing a quality product in the competitive fast-food industry. Chick-fil-A is one of the fastest-growing chains nationally, currently with nearly two billion dollars in annual sales.

One of the defining distinctions of Chick-fil-A is that the restaurants are not open on Sundays. From the time Truett Cathy, the company's founder, started in the restaurant business in 1946, he believed that God wanted him to honor the Sabbath by keeping the stores closed on Sundays. Although he was challenged on this idea many times by shopping mall operators, Truett always held that "we will have more sales in six days than those who are open for seven." This has proven to be true, and today it is no longer an issue to fulfill the malls' requirement to remain open on Sunday.

When you go to a Chick-fil-A restaurant, you can tell something is different about the people and the atmosphere. The messages in the company's kids' meals always reinforce education, values and integrity. Although the employees do not wear their faith on their sleeve, the fruit of the company is known by many—especially the many young restaurant employees who receive educational scholarships each year. The company also focuses on character-building programs for kids, on foster homes and on other community services. I have spoken at Chick-fil-A's corporate headquarters several times and have met with Truett and his son, Dan, and the appearance of their headquarters conveys a sense of quality without extravagance.

Another influential company is HomeBanc, an Atlanta-based mortgage company that is one of the largest mortgage lenders in the Southeast. Pat Flood, the company's CEO, asserts that HomeBanc's financial success is driven by associate satisfaction. Every decision is guided by a simple formula: Happy Associates=Happy Customers=Increased Market Share=Increased Profitability.

HomeBanc's quick growth was causing it to lose touch with the very culture driving its success. When Pat saw this happening—when he no longer knew the names of the associates he met in the elevator—he moved quickly to set up the Office of People and Culture. That's when the company hired "Ike" Reighard, a 52-year-old founding pastor of a

3000-member church, to be HomeBanc's Chief People Officer.

HomeBanc's innovative approach to employee relations and its commitment to excellence have resulted in much-deserved recognition. The company was voted one of the best places to work in 2004 by the *Atlanta Business Chronicle* and by *Atlanta Magazine* and was named "2003 Corporation of the Year" by the Georgia Hispanic Chamber of Commerce. The *Orlando Sentinel* proclaimed HomeBanc to be one of the "100 Best Companies for Working Families" and *Jacksonville Magazine* honored it as one of the "Top 25 Companies Who Care." On the national front, HomeBanc has appeared two years in a row on the *Fortune* magazine list of the "100 Best Companies to Work for," coming it at number 39 in 2004 and at number 20 on the 2005 list.[1]

One of the easiest ways to discredit Christ in the workplace is for Christians to do inferior work. In order to earn respect, our work should stand apart because we do our work unto the Lord (see Col. 3:17). Doing quality work will not be the primary means of winning others to Christ, but doing poor-quality work can disqualify us very quickly from ever having the opportunity to present Christ in a positive light. So go the extra mile when necessary. Make the effort to serve those around you. Do your work with excellence.

Attribute #2: A Foundation of Ethics and Integrity

Sir Arthur Conan Doyle once played a practical joke on 12 respected and well-known men he knew. He sent out 12 telegrams with the same message on each: "Flee at once. All is discovered." Within 24 hours, all 12 men had left the country![2] Obviously, each of these men had something to hide. The cover had suddenly been pulled away to reveal their true natures. The bottom line is that ethics are important.

In December 1983, The Princeton Religion Research Center published a landmark survey conducted for the *Wall Street Journal* by the Gallup Organization. The researchers measured a wide range of moral and ethical behaviors in the workplace, such as calling in sick when not sick, cheating on income taxes and pilfering company supplies for personal use. The results were disappointing, to say the least.

What the researchers found most startling was that there was no significant difference between churched and unchurched people in their ethics and values on the job. In other words, churches seemed to be having little impact on the moral fiber of their people, at least in the workplace. To quote the researchers, "These findings . . . will come as a shock to the religious leaders and underscore the need for religious leaders to channel the new religious interest in America not simply into religious involvement but in deep spiritual commitment."[3]

We have been seeing a wave of ethical failures in the United States since early 2000. In 2002, an article in *Fortune* magazine cited that "Arthur Andersen, Enron, and Salomon Brothers were all brought down, or nearly so, by the rogue actions of a tiny few. But the bad apples in these companies grew and flourished in the same kind of environment: a rotten corporate culture. It's impossible to monitor the actions of every employee, no matter how many accounting and compliance controls you put in place. But either implicitly or explicitly, a company's cultural code is supposed to equip front-line employees to make the right decisions without supervision. Many of the companies that got into trouble revealed a culture engendered with conflicts of interest without safeguards. Rotten cultures produce rotten deeds."[4]

Lack of integrity is nothing new. The Bible is full of examples. One of these involves Gehazi, the assistant to the most famous prophet of his day, Elisha. It's hard to imagine that anyone working with such an anointed man and who saw firsthand the power of God would fail the ethics test. But he did.

When Elisha healed Naaman (a very powerful man in government) from leprosy, he didn't expect to be compensated and he didn't ask for money. When Naaman insisted that Elisha take some form of payment, the prophet answered, "As surely as the Lord lives, whom I serve, I will not accept a thing" (2 Kings 5:16). Gehazi, however, did not agree with his employer. He saw this as a great opportunity for gain and took matters into his own hands. "Gehazi, the servant of Elisha the man of God, said to himself, 'My master was too easy on Naaman, this Aramean, by not accepting from him what he brought. As surely as the Lord lives, I will run after him and get something from him'" (2 Kings 5:20).

As a result of his deception, God judged Gehazi and struck him with leprosy, and his life was never the same. He was removed from serving one of God's most extraordinary prophets.

It is hard to live a life of servanthood and watch others prosper when we ourselves are in need. When our desires and jealousy become so great that we are willing to violate our ethics and integrity, we have moved to a dangerous place. We walk out from under the canopy of God's protection in our lives, saying that His provision is not enough.

I call Psalm 15 the "Ethics Psalm." I particularly like the way *THE MESSAGE* paraphrases it: "God, who gets invited to dinner at your place? How do we get on your guest list? 'Walk straight, act right, tell the truth. Don't hurt your friend, don't blame your neighbor; despise the despicable. Keep your word even when it costs you, make an honest living, never take a bribe. You'll never get blacklisted if you live like this.'"

Each of us has the potential of being a Gehazi if we do not have a foundation built into our lives that makes us willing to receive only what God gives us through the fruit of our obedience.

Attribute #3: Extravagant Love and Service

A friend told me a true story about one of his closest friends (I'll call him Max) who experienced great suffering for the extravagant love he demonstrated to his boss. Max worked on a cargo ship, and his boss was his captain. Max was a good worker, but his boss hated and ridiculed him because of his faith in Christ. Max often shared his faith in Christ with others, and one day, he led the captain's girlfriend to Christ. When she became a Christian, she stopped sleeping with the captain.

This made the captain furious, and he later approached Max while he was at lunch and began beating him. Max did not fight back. The captain proceeded to beat him to a pulp. However, when two other men saw what was taking place, they jumped the sea captain and began beating him in turn. The sea captain was beaten so badly that he needed immediate medical attention.

When Max saw the condition of the sea captain, he came to his aid and began helping him. The sea captain was so moved that Max would do that after he had beaten him up that he began to weep, unable to understand what could move a man to have such love in the face of a beating. The sea captain accepted Jesus at that moment.

The Bible tells us that while we were yet sinners, Christ came and paid our penalty so that we might live eternally. Many in the workplace have never known the love of Christ. You might be the only one they ever meet who can introduce them to this love. "Whoever wants to become great among you must be your servant, and whoever wants to be first must be your slave—just as the Son of Man did not come to be served, but to serve, and to give his life as a ransom for many" (Matt. 20:28).

Someone once said, "people do not care what you know until they know that you care."[5] When you genuinely take an interest in another person in the workplace, you become a credible person in his or her eyes. You stand out among the crowd.

Recently, I took a phone call from a CEO of a company who shared about the impact of the *TGIF* devotionals that a family member had been sending him. I recognized that the man was not a Christian. Though I was leaving town that afternoon and was pressed for time, we began to talk, and ultimately the man prayed over the phone to receive Christ. Later, he commented on how impressed he was that I took the time to listen to him even though I had to get out of town. Being a busy executive, this man equated time with love and service. That is what the world is looking for.

Attribute #4: Signs and Wonders

The fourth attribute of an effective workplace witness is signs and wonders. The Early Church made a huge impact on society not through knowledge, ethics, or service alone, but through demonstrating the power of God. "The apostles performed many miraculous signs and wonders among the people" (Acts 5:12).

Jesus gave His workplace apostles the anointing that allowed them to perform miraculous signs. "I tell you the truth, anyone who has faith in me will do what I have been doing. He will do even greater things than these, because I am going to the Father" (John 14:12). Unfortunately, most Christians in the workplace today do not realize God desires to reveal Himself in miraculous ways in their workplaces. We have been satisfied to have the gospel but deny its power.

God is raising up a new kind of workplace believer who is experiencing the power of God in daily work life. One of these wonderful workplace Christians is Emeka Nywankpa, a barrister (lawyer) in Nigeria. Emeka spoke at a conference a few years ago on the subject of how the spiritual impacts the physical.

Emeka shared a story about arguing a big Supreme Court case in his country. There were five points to argue in the case. The morning the trial began, he prayed with his wife and junior lawyers in his chambers. During his prayer time, he sensed that the Holy Spirit was telling him, "Do not argue points one through four. Only argue point five."

In the courtroom, Emeka announced that he wished to drop points one through four and only wished to argue point five. The judge was shocked, but gave him permission to proceed. He argued point five and sat down. The other attorney got up, and then for twelve minutes stumbled around trying to defend his position, unable to get a coherent word out. Finally, he approached the bench and said, "Your Lordship, it is unfortunate that my learned friend has dropped the first four points. I wish to yield the case." The other attorney had only prepared for the first four points. Emeka won the case. God had given him a strategy to win his case supernaturally. It made no sense to him, but he obeyed and God gave him victory in a very unusual way.

Chuck Ripka lives in Elk River, Minnesota, a community of about 20,000 people 40 miles outside of Minneapolis. Chuck and some business leaders opened a bank in 2003 with the intent to use the bank as a place of ministry. Within the first 18 months of the bank's opening, Chuck and his staff saw more than 70 people accept salvation inside the bank, and there were numerous physical healings. The bank employees offer prayer for their customers in the boardroom and often pray for those who come to the teller windows. There is excitement in the bank each day about what God is going to do.

I often receive requests from the media for interviews about the Faith at Work movement. One day, the *New York Times Magazine* called. After several subsequent conversations, the reporter said, "I believe I have a good understanding of this Faith at Work movement, but can you point me to someone who can demonstrate what this looks like in a daily workplace?" I told the writer to give Chuck Ripka a call.

Chuck immediately began praying for the writer after I told him the reporter would be calling him. A few days later, Chuck called me and said the Lord was going to use this article not only for the workplace movement, but also for this writer's life. He even had the boldness to tell the writer that when he called.

The writer visited Chuck and the bank for two days. He went with Chuck everywhere—he had dinner in Chuck's home, attended community meetings, interviewed all the employees of the bank, and watched Chuck pray for many people at the bank. The writer was impressed that this was the real deal.

At the end of the reporter's visit, Chuck and his friend Larry Ihle asked if they could pray for God's blessing on him. He agreed, and they prayed for God's blessing on his writing skills and for the *New York Times*. They prayed that God would help him write the article. The writer was touched by this. Afterward, Chuck asked him about his own relationship with God, which led to him praying to receive Christ. Two weeks later, photographers came to take pictures for the article, and they too prayed to receive Christ.

When the article came out October 31, 2004, it was one of the best and most extensive articles on the Faith at Work movement that has been written from a secular viewpoint. Chuck has stayed in contact with the writer, and the two have become good friends. God has opened many doors as a result, and the secular media has taken note of this growing movement. Since then, Chuck has had interviews with the *London Times*, a broadcast network from France and Germany, a Hong Kong newspaper and many city newspapers across the United States.

Excellence, ethics and integrity, extravagant love and service, and signs and wonders—these are the attributes of the worker that God is using in dramatic ways. May the Lord allow you to make these four qualities part of the makeup of your own workplace.

How About You?

1. List each of the four attributes discussed in this chapter. Rank yourself in each attribute on a scale of 1-10.
2. Name one thing you can do better in each area that will make you a more effective Christian worker.

CHAPTER 5

FOUR TYPES OF CHRISTIANS

But if you are led by the Spirit, you are not under the law.

GALATIANS 5:18

Think for a moment about Christians who have made the most significant impact on the world for Jesus in the past 100 years. Make a mental list of four or five people who immediately come to mind.

How many of those were full-time vocational ministry workers and how many were workplace Christians? My guess is that your list is made up mostly of vocational ministry workers—people like Billy Graham, Rees Howells, George Mueller, Bill Bright, D. L. Moody or even Mother Teresa.

My point is this: Where are the men and women of faith from the workplace? Why aren't we seeing them on the list? Absent are men like Jeremiah Lanphier, a New York businessman whose prayer efforts sparked a nationwide revival; R. G. LeTourneau, an American construction company owner who influenced many for Christ; William Wilberforce, an English statesman who dedicated his life to abolishing slavery; Arthur Guinness, an entrepreneur and founder of Guinness Beer, whose work had a major effect on society in Ireland and England; or Brigid, a fifth-century Irish woman who helped an estimated 13,000 people escape from poverty and slavery into Christian service and industry.

George Barna says that 40 percent of the American population claims to be born-again.[1] If your company had such a high percentage of the market share of your industry, don't you think it would have a lot of influence? Coca-Cola has a 40 percent market share in the soft drink industry. Do they carry a lot of clout and influence? You bet they do.

The reason Christians are not at the top of the list of those who make an impact on the world around them is because most believers are not embracing their workplace calling. In his book *Anointed for Business*, Ed Silvoso provides a thoughtful look at the four types of Christians in the workplace. The following four categories provide an excellent tool for self-assessment:

1. The Christian who is simply trying to survive.
2. The Christian who is living by Christian principles.
3. The Christian who is living by the power of the Holy Spirit.
4. The Christian who is transforming his or her workplaces for Christ.[2]

I had studied these four types of Christians for many years without grouping them into these four categories, as Silvoso has done. Allow me to expand upon each category.

Category #1: The Christian Who Is Simply Trying to Survive

Christians who are simply trying to survive have no purpose or zeal for integrating their faith at work. They have not seen the power or presence of God in their work lives. Solomon describes such people: "So my heart began to despair over all my toilsome labor under the sun. . . . What does a man get for all the toil and anxious striving with which he labors under the sun? All his days his work is pain and grief; even at night his mind does not rest. This too is meaningless" (Eccles. 2:20,22-23).

Such Christians segment their faith life from their work life. They lack purpose and meaning and they have little direction. Most likely, their work is reduced to collecting a paycheck at the end of the week. They have never heard the voice of God, especially not at work, and they would never consider praying at work or for a workplace-related issue. Even though they go to church, they see it as an obligation to do something for God. In the final analysis, these individuals are defeated Christians who are simply trying to survive. The world is full of these surviving Christians who are waiting for the lifeboat of salvation to take them off this "evil" planet.

Category #2: The Christian Who Is Living by Christian Principles

The second type of Christians in the workplace includes those who are living by Christian principles. Americans love programs and systems to do things. We participate in 12-step programs and read books with guaranteed formulas to help us lose weight or improve our marriages. This programmed teaching can be beneficial. It gives people a track to run on. Let's face it, if the whole world lived on Christian principles, we would definitely have a better world. However, it is important to recognize that the root of this type of teaching comes largely from a Greek-based system for attaining knowledge, as compared to the Early Church Hebraic model of experiential learning.

The Hebrews preferred to learn wisdom through obedience, not through reason and analysis. Teachers taught their students more by modeling life experience than by conveying information, and the students had a process-oriented way of learning that appealed to the heart and resulted in the active participation of the disciple. The Hebraic style relied on the personal touch of a leader as a facilitator. It enabled believers in the Early Church to become doers of the Word, not hearers or learners only. The end result of the Early-Church instruction was an active, mature love that motivated the believers to serve others.

In the second and third centuries, as more and more Greek scholars came into the faith, they influenced the Early Church with teaching methodologies that focused on reason, logic and oratory skills. The Greek way of learning tended to be program-based and often took place in large, impersonal groups. The Greeks emphasized do's and don'ts and logical principles, and they expected students to accumulate a repository of data.[3]

One of the primary reasons that many of us don't have much of an impact on our world is because so many of us are byproducts of this Greek system of education. In the Church, this approach eliminates the supernatural because it depends so heavily on logic and reason rather than living by the power of the Holy Spirit and being led by God. Paul warned against the Greek influence in his letter to the Corinthians, where he stated, "My message and my preaching were not with wise and persuasive words, but with a demonstration of the Spirit's power, so that your faith might not rest on men's wisdom, but on God's power" (1 Cor. 2:4-5).

Christians who are living by principles tend to be ethical people who want to do the right thing. However, if we only live by ethics, we will never experience the power of God. (On the other hand, if we fail the ethics test, we will be disqualified from power encounters with God and fail to be a witness to the world.) In order to experience the freedom and power of God in the Holy Spirit, Christians must move beyond the "milk" of programmed Christianity to an intimate relationship with Jesus. That is where they will experience the power of God.

Category #3: The Christian Who Is Living by the Power of the Holy Spirit

Christians who are living by the power of the Holy Spirit have a heart toward God and seek Him about every aspect of their lives. They understand the importance of developing a heart toward God through prayer, study of the Word of God and obedience. They realize that these are the three core ingredients to experiencing the power of God in their lives.

To illustrate these types of Christians, let me tell you about Doug, one of our close friends and board members. One busy day, Doug went to the airport, barely made his flight and found his assigned seat in economy class. As the doors shut, he suddenly heard his name called out. He was being upgraded to first class. Because he had never flown with the airline before, he wondered how in the world he got upgraded.

He ended up sitting next to a well-dressed man who was apparently successful and wealthy, but who seemed to be very irritated. As Doug pondered what God might do with this situation (which seemed to have been divinely orchestrated), he quietly prayed, "Lord, tell me something about this man so that he would know that You know him." Immediately the words "finance" and "financial services" popped into his mind.

Doug now had to decide whether this was God answering his prayer or just his own thoughts. Though he was not used to doing things like this, he decided to take a risk, assume it was God and go for it. Turning to the man he said, "I understand you are in financial services."

The man looked at him and said, "Yes I am. But how in the world would *you* know that?"

Doug was just as amazed as the man was. "Do you really want to know how I know that?" he asked.

"Yes, I would," the man replied.

Doug explained that when he sat down, he had prayed and asked God to tell him something about him. "God told me specifically that you were in financial services," he said.

The man, startled and not sure what to make of this, began a conversation with Doug. It turns out he was the CEO of one of the largest financial services companies in the United States—a 32 billion dollar company with global influence. Doug spent the rest of the flight talking with the man about the integration of faith with work and business.

The man did not accept Christ, but he experienced a touch of God in a very personal way that may be a stepping-stone for him to come into the Kingdom in the future. It was a supernatural seed-planting encounter that encouraged Doug to be open to the Holy Spirit at a greater level.

Another illustration comes from an experience in my own life. When I published my first *TGIF* devotional book, part of the publishing agreement was that I would purchase 1,000 of the copies myself. I figured I could quickly resell the books, but after six months we had sold only a few books a week. We had no real distribution system in place, and I was concerned. Then I felt the Lord prompting me to do something in faith.

In Mark 11:22-24, Jesus states, "Have faith in God . . . I tell you the truth, if anyone says to this mountain, 'Go, throw yourself into the sea,' and does not doubt in his heart but believes that what he says will happen, it will be done for him." I told Angie I felt we needed to put Mark 11 into practice and speak to the books to leave our basement. So we laid hands on the boxes of books and told them to leave! We told our mountain of books to get into the hands of people where they could make a difference. Believe me, we felt very foolish. However, we did it out of obedience.

A few hours later, I received a phone call from a ministry in Dallas, Texas, which ordered 300 books from us. The amazing thing was that it was a Saturday! We sold more books in one transaction than we had in six months. The Lord built our faith through this experience.

Sometimes, God wants us to exercise the authority that He has given us in the spiritual realm. This does not mean that God is our genie and we can simply command Him to do things at our whim. God must lead us into these actions. But many of us never even think outside the box enough to give God this opportunity because we don't know that this power is available to us.

Paul understood that it was not knowledge that would change the world but the power of God working through believers. You and I need to move at this dimension if we are going to transform the workplace. Everything we do should be led by the power of the Holy Spirit in our lives.

Category #4: The Christian Who Is Transforming His or Her Workplace for Christ

A wonderful byproduct of living by the power of the Holy Spirit is that you can transform your workplace for God. Christians who passionately seek the manifestation of God's kingdom here on Earth will be able to realize this transformation in their workplaces. Jesus talked about the kingdom of God 70 times in the New Testament—more often than he mentioned salvation. While salvation is part of bringing the kingdom of God on Earth, it includes much more. When the kingdom of God is demonstrated on Earth, it can transform the workplace and society.

As a young believer at the turn of the century, Arthur Guinness walked the streets of Ireland and despaired over the alcoholism in his country. Hard liquor was the choice of drink in his day. Arthur cried out to God for a solution. "God, you must do something about the drunkenness on the streets of Ireland!" At that moment, he sensed that God gave him an answer—an answer that surprised him. The thought that came to his mind was *make a drink that men will drink that will be good for them.*

So Arthur created a dark, stout beer called Guinness. It was indeed a drink "that men will drink that will be good for them," for it was so full of minerals and natural trace elements that even pregnant women could benefit from its high iron content. It was also nearly impossible for people to get drunk on Guinness beer because it was so heavy that it was difficult to drink more than a couple of pints. In addition, it had a fairly low alcohol level at the time. (The recipe has changed recently and it now has a slightly higher alcohol content.)

The answer to Arthur's prayer became the national drink in Ireland. Arthur was elevated to the House of Lords because of his philanthropy and wealth, and he used his success to fund an orphanage in Ireland and to change the judicial system in Great Britain. Arthur Guinness is a great example of a working Christian who helped transform his nation.[4]

On January 23, 2005, Victor Yushenko was sworn in as the president of Ukraine. Following his inauguration, Yushenko invited all Ukrainian Christian denominations to join him in public prayer and blessing for the nation. "This is a totally new thing for our nation," said Sunday Adelaja, pastor of the Embassy of the Blessed Kingdom of God for All Nations, in Kiev, the largest church in Europe. "Remember, Ukraine is a former Communist society."

Yushenko then selected Yulia Timoshenko, a born-again and Spirit-filled believer, as prime minister. At the Oath of Office for the new prime minister on February 3, 2005, President Yushenko again shocked the nation by taking a clear and unprecedented stand against corruption. In his address, Yushenko stated that his government would not steal from the public, would not give or receive bribes and would never use money to shift lobby votes. He promised that he would take full responsibility for the actions of his government and demanded that the principles of openness, transparency and uprightness filter throughout every department and cabinet. "No decision should be taken in secret," Yushenko said. "Everything must be done openly and in public view."

In her address, Prime Minister Timoshenko made one simple point: "Our government has come to the conclusion that Ukraine can never rise on her feet until she bows her knees before the Almighty God." Shortly thereafter, Timoshenko surprised the members of Parliament by outlining a new program of reform for the nation based upon the following biblical concepts of national transformation:

• Faith (in God, the nation and individual citizens)
• Justice (to build an upright society)
• Harmony (between citizens and leaders)
• Security (of individual people, national interests and properties)
• Life (abundant life in every sphere through social programs)
• World Relations (that Ukraine would integrate itself as a European nation, cultivating good relations with other countries, including Russia and the European Union)

When Timoshenko announced the new Ministers of Parliament, "We as believers couldn't help but laugh," said Adelja, "because of who was placed at the head of the [Ukrainian KGB]: Alexander Turshinov. This man, a believer, grew up in a Baptist family during the Communist regime. The top assignment of the KGB at that time was to destroy religion and faith, Baptists and Evangelicals in particular. Now, the head of this dreaded organization is a man who believes in the very thing they tried to destroy. Yes, God has a sense of humor!"[5]

If God can transform the foundations of an ungodly nation, just think what He could do in your workplace! Start asking God to help you see how to transform your workplace today.

How About You?

1. Which category of Christian best describes you? Explain.
2. If you said the first or second category, what more do you need to do to become a Christian living by the power of the Holy Spirit?

CHAPTER 6

THE RELIGIOUS SPIRIT AND THE WORKPLACE

For our struggle is not against flesh and blood, but against the rulers,
against the authorities, against the powers of this dark world and against
the spiritual forces of evil in the heavenly realms.

EPHESIANS 6:12

As believers begin to express the life of Christ in their work lives, they need to be aware of another set of Satan's deceptions, namely, the religious spirit and spiritual strongholds. Though this is a new concept in the Faith at Work category, we need to be aware of them so we are not hindered from walking in power and freedom in our workplace calling. The workplace is the last place Satan wants to see Jesus. The business sector has a huge capacity to influence every sphere of society, so it would make sense that the enemy would do everything in his power to keep that from happening.

Dr. Peter Wagner defines the religious spirit as "an agent of Satan assigned to prevent change and maintain the status quo by using religious devices."[1] The religious spirit seeks to distort a genuine move of God through deception, control and manipulation. This spirit operates out of old religious structures and attempts to maintain the status quo, favoring tradition over a genuine, intimate relationship with God. It influences believers to live the Christian life based on works instead of grace. Similar to the Greek way of thinking, the religious spirit depends on human effort to acquire spiritual knowledge and favor from God. Dr. Wagner explains that the religious spirit's primary strategy is as follows:

> The spirit of religion's primary strategy here is to promote the idea that belonging to a Christian church or doing religious things is what saves you. It succeeds if it can, for example, persuade Catholics to think that they can be saved by lighting candles to Mary, or Baptists to think that they can be saved by going to church every Sunday and by carrying a Bible, or Lutherans to think they are saved if they have been baptized and confirmed. . . . It does not allow believers to move on to receive the filling of the Holy Spirit or freedom in Christ, or to enter into God's full destiny for their lives. Paul specifically warns that the devil, by his craftiness, can corrupt *minds* and keep them from "the simplicity that is in Christ" (2 Cor. 11:3).[2]

In the years before the Protestant Reformation, Martin Luther's greatest challenge was to root out the religious spirit. He was told by his religious teachers that there were stringent requirements for receiving the favor of God. "Remember Martin, just to pray by yourself is not enough. The church has to pray for you too. Even when the priest has asked that you be forgiven, God will not listen unless you do good works. The more gifts you give to the church and to the poor, the more trips you make to Rome and Jerusalem, the more pleasures you give up, the better will be your chances for heaven. The best and safest way to do all this, and the one that is most God pleasing, is to give up everything and become a monk."[3] The essence of Martin Luther's struggle to win God's favor still resides in many a Christian worker.

We must realize that we are not dealing with flesh and blood when we deal with the religious spirit. The religious spirit deceives believers into thinking that the only way to get God's approval is through works.

It nullifies the importance of faith and grace that has been given to them through the work of the Cross.

The Religious Spirit in the New Testament

In the New Testament, the Galatians started their Christian life simply by believing and having faith in God. However, somewhere along the road, they were influenced to live their lives by focusing on rules and regulations and to live according to their own human effort. Read the apostle Paul's words as he confronted the believers in Galatia about the effect of the religious spirit on their lives:

> You foolish Galatians! Who has bewitched you? Before your very eyes Jesus Christ was clearly portrayed as crucified. I would like to learn just one thing from you: Did you receive the Spirit *by observing the law,* or by believing what you heard? Are you so foolish? After beginning with the Spirit, are you now trying to attain your goal by *human effort?* Have you suffered so much for nothing—if it really was for nothing? Does God give you his Spirit and work miracles among you because you observe the law, or because you *believe* what you heard? (Gal. 3:1-5, emphasis added).

Living according to rules and regulations and by our own human efforts is a trap set by the religious spirit that we can all fall into. However, it is not the abundant life that Jesus promised (see John 10:10). In Galatians 2:20-21, Paul describes how we should live our lives: "I have been crucified with Christ and I no longer live, but Christ lives in me. The life I live in the body, *I live by faith in the Son of God,* who loved me and gave himself for me. *I do not set aside the grace of God,* for if righteousness could be gained through the law, Christ died for nothing!" (emphasis added).

In the Gospel of Matthew, we also read about a rich young ruler who was prevented from making a commitment to the one true God because of the religious spirit. Although he considered himself religious because he followed the laws, he had an idol in his life that prevented him from making a total or "sold-out" commitment to Jesus.

Now a man came up to Jesus and asked, "Teacher, what good thing must I do to get eternal life?"

"Why do you ask me about what is good?" Jesus replied. "There is only One who is good. If you want to enter life, obey the commandments."

"Which ones?" the man inquired.

Jesus replied, "'Do not murder, do not commit adultery, do not steal, do not give false testimony, honor your father and mother,' and 'love your neighbor as yourself.'"

"All these I have kept," the young man said. "What do I still lack?"

Jesus answered, "If you want to be perfect, go, sell your possessions and give to the poor, and you will have treasure in heaven. Then come, follow me."

When the young man heard this, he went away sad, because he had great wealth (Matt. 19:16-22).

The rich young ruler wanted to gain God's approval on his own terms by fulfilling the law. However, Jesus cut through the religious spirit by speaking to the heart of his issue.

When the Early Church expanded its leadership, it commissioned Stephen, a man full of faith and the Holy Spirit, to active ministry. "The word of God spread. The number of disciples in Jerusalem increased rapidly, and a large number of priests became obedient to the faith. Now Stephen, a man full of God's grace and power, did great wonders and miraculous signs among the people" (Acts 6:7-8). Notice how Stephen began to make an impact on his city—by performing signs and wonders. However, his work also stirred up the religious spirit, and Stephen became the first person martyred for his faith.

The Religious Spirit in the Workplace

The religious spirit discourages a genuine move of God and will thwart the activity of God under the banner of religious righteousness and dogma. It also motivates believers to live out their faith in legalistic and rigid ways. We need to be aware of how this happens in a workplace calling. Here are some characteristics of how the religious spirit manifests itself in believers in workplace situations:

- They may have difficulty praying and applying God's promises to everyday work encounters.
- They may believe that biblical truths apply only to their personal lives, families and churches, not to their jobs.
- They may focus on evangelizing coworkers, but fail to do their work with excellence.
- They may give greater priority to religious activity and events than to relationships with others at work.
- They maintain a "we" or "I" versus "them" attitude when relating to non-Christians in the workplace.
- They may refuse to join a workplace prayer group or Bible study because they feel that it is trying to replace the role of a particular local church. They don't see a need for such activity in the workplace. They feel the need to compartmentalize faith activities to their local church alone.
- They discount the idea that Christianity could transform a workplace, city or nation as "overzealous," "naïve" or even doctrinally wrong.

The following is a quick self-assessment checklist that you can use to reveal the influence of the religious spirit's involvement in your life. Place a check by any item with which you can identify.

Religious Spirit Self-Assessment

- ☐ You believe your faith life should remain separate from your work life.
- ☐ You're motivated to share Christ out of duty.
- ☐ You can't relate to non-believers because you're afraid of rejection.
- ☐ You display a "better than they are" attitude toward nonbelievers.
- ☐ You are viewed by others as dogmatic and rigid (not simply a person of conviction).
- ☐ You feel compelled to be involved in religious activity and you can't relax in your faith.
- ☐ You often feel guilty (not the same as the conviction of the Holy Spirit) for not sharing Christ with others.
- ☐ You often engage in religious debate.
- ☐ You need a packaged presentation in order to share the gospel.
- ☐ When talking about spiritual matters to strangers, you tend to talk about your church or ask about their church involvement versus talking about Jesus and their personal relationship with God.
- ☐ You have a difficult time socializing, loving or accepting those who do not believe the way you do.
- ☐ You are motivated by your church leadership out of guilt and Christian duty instead of loving devotion to Christ.
- ☐ You discourage change, preferring religious tradition.
- ☐ You believe that the ministry gifts listed in 1 Corinthians 12 and 14 and Ephesians 4:11 are no longer applicable today; or, if you believe they are valid, you think that they are for religious professionals, not for you.
- ☐ You form relationships for the purpose of achieving a religious activity rather than developing community from which Christ-like ministry flows naturally.
- ☐ Your loyalty to denominational structures is greater than your commitment to the kingdom of God and the entire Body of Christ.
- ☐ You view government as an "evil empire" from which we must separate instead of influence for good.
- ☐ You don't see the need to work with other Christian ministry groups in a common effort; you usually feel that your way is the primary way and everyone should join your endeavor so as to not compromise your belief or doctrine.

Spiritual Strongholds

The apostle Paul enlists the word "stronghold" to define the spiritual fortresses where Satan and his legions go for protection. These fortresses exist in the thought-patterns and ideas that govern individuals in their homes, workplaces and churches, as well as in communities and nations. Before victory can be claimed, these strongholds must be pulled down. Only then can the mighty weapons of the Word and the Spirit effectively plunder Satan's house. As Paul states,

> The weapons we fight with are not the weapons of the world. On the contrary, they have divine power to demolish strongholds. We demolish arguments and every pretension that sets itself up against the knowledge of God, and we take captive every thought to make it obedient to Christ (2 Cor. 10:4-5).

Here is an example of how a stronghold can develop and affect someone's working life. "Jerry" had grown up with a father who was successful and a workaholic. Although Jerry lacked for nothing materially, he felt a lack of closeness to his parents and had difficulty sharing his feelings with others as an adult. When Jerry was still in his early teens, his father died very suddenly. His large family was left with little support, and insecurity and fear became the dominating factors in the young man's life.

Vowing to himself that he would never again suffer financial need, Jerry worked hard at his business in his adult life, putting stress on many personal and business relationships. He became very successful.

His relationship with God was seen as a model among his peers, but when examined closer, there was something that just wasn't right. He often displayed anger in stressful situations and he would shame his employees into correcting their behaviors. Jerry had little accountability beyond his clients. A pattern began to emerge that motivated Jerry to place restrictions on those around him when they failed in the financial area. Finally, Jerry's marriage disintegrated and some major crises in his business led to financial difficulties.

However, through the counsel of some trusted friends who had an understanding of spiritual strongholds, Jerry came to realize that underneath some of these symptoms, a religious stronghold of insecurity and fear had been established. To reduce his anxiety level, Jerry (and his father and grandfather before him) had worked hard to control people and circumstances.

As the Holy Spirit convicted him of sins he had committed against people in his life, Jerry sought forgiveness and made restitution. His priorities shifted to God and family first, followed by close friends and business. God began to show Jerry that he could have true intimacy with God and others when these underlying strongholds were removed. Jerry became a new person, and for the first time he experienced a degree of intimacy and freedom in his walk with God. Today, Jerry sees the hand of God restoring all aspects of his life and can testify to God's miraculous hand in many of his everyday experiences in life and work.

I am pleased to tell you that I am Jerry. It is from first-hand experience that I can discuss the effect of spiritual strongholds that can plague our personal lives and, inevitably, our work lives.

Generational Strongholds

By reading between the lines in the first two chapters of Genesis, as well as elsewhere in the Bible, we find that God created us with seven needs: (1) dignity, (2) authority, (3) blessing and provision, (4) security, (5) purpose and meaning, (6) freedom and boundaries, and (7) love and companionship. Whenever we seek to meet one or more of these basic needs outside God's design, we have set the stage for the development of a generational stronghold.[4]

God wants to release the full measure of His love in our lives, so that we no longer need to operate out of old strongholds. In Ephesians 3:16-18, Paul prayed that we would experience this fullness:

I pray that out of his glorious riches he may strengthen you with power through his Spirit in your inner being, so that Christ may dwell in your hearts through faith. And I pray that you, being rooted and established in love, may have power, together with all the saints, to grasp how wide and long and high and deep is the love of Christ, and to know this love that surpasses knowledge—that you may be filled to the measure of all the fullness of God.

When I came into a greater understanding of the operation of spiritual strongholds, I did a thorough study of my family history. I interviewed family members to see what I could learn about the way my father and grandfather related to God and their families. I studied their work habits. I found that each of us had the same symptoms:

- a need for recognition from performance (civic projects, sports, business success)
- an emphasis on building financial security (we were workaholics)
- a lack of emotional intimacy
- a works-based relationship toward God
- a tendency to over-control people and circumstances

This was an amazing discovery for me. For the first time, I realized this stronghold had affected three generations of my family. I was being given the opportunity to break this generational stronghold through the power of Christ so that it would not get passed down any further.

Strongholds work at the subconscious level and are not easily recognized until a major crisis in a person's life forces him or her to look deeper at the root causes of the problem. I learned that one root of the religious spirit is control. Man does not want to give up control over his life, so he creates controlled systems designed to make him feel acceptable by God. Again, this is a works-based attempt to gain God's favor, which invalidates the work of the Cross. The sequence of how these strongholds develop in an individual is as follows:

1. Satanic-inspired *thoughts* are introduced into the person's mind.
2. The individual entertains these thoughts, which bring out *emotions*.

3. Giving in to these emotions eventually leads the person to take some sort of *action*.

4. Continual participation in the action causes the individual to develop a *habit*.

5. As the habit develops, a *stronghold* is built.[5]

Imagine being born with a pair of sunglasses on. You would grow up looking at the world through those sunglasses. You would never know that you could see better without the sunglasses unless someone revealed this to you. Now imagine taking those glasses off for the first time and seeing the inside of a room much brighter and clearer. Strongholds operate this way. They masquerade as if they are part of our personality, and we accept them for our whole life. However, the truth is that Jesus wants to totally renew our minds and hearts. Strongholds keep us from getting restored.

Renouncing the Religious Spirit and Spiritual Strongholds

Nearly all of us struggle to some degree with a religious spirit and spiritual strongholds. But God does not want us to continue to be ruled by them or to impose them upon anyone else. If you recognize that you are operating under the influence of a religious spirit or a stronghold, renounce it in prayer, repent for what you've done, ask God's forgiveness and the forgiveness of others, and resist the return of the spirit or stronghold. Receive God's power to forsake it, and ask Him to make you sensitive to the times when you are tempted to act in a wrong spirit. Move into freedom by asking God to fill you afresh with the power of His Holy Spirit.

When you encounter a person who is influenced by a religious spirit or a stronghold, let your first response be prayer. Ask God for wisdom and love and for Him to set the person free. If the person has offended you, forgive him or her and don't let that person's actions or attitudes keep a grip on you. Let your life be based on a genuine faith rooted in Jesus' life and example.

Most of all, continually become transformed by the renewing of your mind, as we are told to do in Romans 12:2. This is your best insurance against any spiritual influences that do not come from God. As you develop a strong relationship with God through the power of His Spirit, not only will you become empowered to bring the Kingdom to those around you at work, but also you will be able to resist Satan's sabotage.

How About You?

1. Do you see ways in which the religious spirit has affected your life? Give some examples.
2. If you find that you have allowed the religious spirit to operate in your life, you will want to renounce this through a prayer of repentance along the lines of the following prayer:

Father, I hereby renounce the spirit of religion that I have allowed to operate in my life. In the name of Jesus, I accept the grace that You have bestowed on my life through the presence and power of Jesus Christ in my life and through His shed blood on the cross. In Jesus' name I pray. Amen.

CHAPTER 7

BRINGING GOD TO THE 9 TO 5 WINDOW

A man can do nothing better than to eat and drink and find satisfaction in his work.
ECCLESIASTES 2:24

As you may know, for years Christians have sought to evangelize the largely unreached people groups who live in what is called "The 10/40 Window"—the expanse between the 10th and 40th parallels north of the equator, from Africa through east Asia. But what you might not know is that there's another window that is opening to allow Christians to introduce people to God: the "9 to 5 Window." It's a window of opportunity that's just as exciting.[1]

Angie Tracey, an executive with the Centers for Disease Control (CDC) in Atlanta, Georgia, recalls how God was taken out of the CDC Christmas celebration at her center starting 10 years ago. "First, we had 'Christmas parties'. . . . Then, due to controversy and not wanting to offend anyone, they became 'holiday parties.' Three years ago, it was determined that the term 'holiday' was offensive because it still reminded people of Christmas, so they were renamed 'Snowflake Festivals.'"

However, things have changed today.

Around the time the Snowflake Festival was introduced, God put an idea on Angie's heart: to create an opportunity for Christians to fellowship on the job. She thought perhaps this could happen through a prayer breakfast or a devotional luncheon. She would have been glad if 15 or 20 employees came. But God had something more in mind.

Within 24 hours of the official announcement that the management had approved the agency's first Christian employee association, the Christian Fellowship Group, she received over 200 calls and e-mails from employees wanting to participate. At first, many of the callers were asking her if it was really true that they could have a Bible at their desk and gather in a conference room at lunch for Bible studies. She found that there were employees who were actually going to the basement to read their Bibles during their lunch hours so that no one would say anything to them!

Today, however, there has been a major change. Christians and non-Christians stop by her office to ask her to pray for them or their family members. Christians contact her about how to handle a workplace problem from a biblical perspective. God is moving throughout her workplace. Today the group membership is approaching 400 people, with eight standing committees and an executive committee, and coordinators and Bible studies at many CDC locations across the country. Stories similar to Angie's have been surfacing at a rapid pace in the past five years.

An Overview of the Faith at Work Movement

Many leaders involved in reaching the 9 to 5 Window refer to this move of God as the Faith at Work movement. The secular media has been one of the first to recognize its impact.

In November 1999, *Business Week* reported that five years ago, only one conference on spirituality in the workplace could be identified; now there are hundreds. The article also reported that there are more than 10,000 Bible studies and prayer groups in workplaces that meet regularly.[2] Two years later, *Fortune* affirmed the existence of the movement in a cover story titled "God and Business," reporting the marketplace presence of "a mostly unorganized mass of believers—a counterculture bubbling up all over corporate America—who want to bridge the traditional divide between spirituality and work." The article went on to say:

> Historically, such folk operated below the radar, on their own or in small workplace groups where they prayed or studied the Bible. But now they are getting organized and going public to agitate for change. People who want to mix God and business are rebels on several fronts. They reject the centuries-old American conviction that spirituality is a private matter. They challenge religious thinkers who disdain business as an inherently impure pursuit. They disagree with business people who say that religion is unavoidably divisive.[3]

In 2004 and 2005, major secular media also did stories on the trend. On October 31, 2004, the *New York Times Magazine* featured a cover story on Christianity in the workplace entitled "With God at Our Desks." The article stated:

> The idea is that Christians have for too long practiced their faith on Sundays and left it behind during the workweek, and that there is a moral vacuum in the modern workplace, which leads to backstabbing careerism, empty routines for employees and CEO's who push for profits at the expense of society, the environment and their fellow human beings.[4]

This story came out just days before George W. Bush was re-elected as president with the largest popular vote ever. This presidential race revealed that the key issue for voters was not the war in Iraq, the economy or healthcare. The defining issue was morals and values.

Subsequent features have appeared in the *London Times, Boston Globe,* CBS morning news, the BBC, *Atlanta Journal,* CNN, National Public Radio, *Los Angeles Times*, and the *Charlotte Observer,* to name just a few. On March 31, 2005, CNBC aired a one-hour story on faith at work. The international media has also taken note with stories or features appearing in major media in Hong Kong, Germany, England and France.

In the wake of these articles and features, the Christian media has also highlighted the Faith at Work movement, with stories appearing in *New Man Magazine, Charisma, Christianity Today* and *Decision* magazine. Christian leaders are also acknowledging the trend. Henry Blackaby, author of *Experiencing God: Knowing and Doing His Will*, meets regularly with CEOs of Fortune 500 companies to discuss what it means to bring Christ into a corporate environment. He observes, "I've never seen the activity of God this deeply in the business community as I do right now."[5]

Kent Humphreys, a business owner and president of Fellowship of Companies for Christ, a ministry devoted to serving executives and CEOs, wholeheartedly agrees with such assessments. "Leaders in the workplace from every part of the country are experiencing a hunger to be involved and they're searching the web to find those who are of like heart. Those who are a little further along in the movement understand the principle, but are now more anxious for training and practical helps of what it looks like in their workplace."

The Faith at Work movement is not just an American phenomenon, nor is it only happening among business executives. Brenda deCharmoy, the business consultant from South Africa mentioned in chapter 2, remarks: "I am beginning to see more and more people and churches becoming aware that the workplace is a key area for God and we should give it more attention. I think the tide has built quite a lot this last year. There is more questioning by workplace people of the issue of God in their 9 to 5 time. I also see more leaders realizing that going to church and leaving God behind does not work in the end."

One subscriber to my daily e-mail devotional, *TGIF, Today God Is First,* summed it up well: "I never really considered my secular work as a ministry until I read your (devotional) . . . now I feel I have as much a ministry as my pastor. I simply have a different mission field." People are hungry to know how to effectively integrate their faith life with their work life, and they are energized by the call.

Let's look more closely at this emerging mission field we call the 9 to 5 Window, which in several strategic ways is growing larger each day.

The Movement in Major Companies

Larry Julian, business consultant and author of *God Is My CEO* (which has sold more than 100,000 copies), says he finds an incredible receptivity in secular corporations to hear what he has to say. "I am seeking more ways to bring my Christian faith into the corporate world where I have spent much of my life. There is an openness that has not been there before."

This openness is partially evidenced by the number of Christian affinity groups that have been birthed in companies within the last five years. The Coca-Cola Christian Fellowship was formed by Steve Hyland in 2002, with 275 people attending the first meeting at their world headquarters. The mission of the fellowship is "to bring together a community of Christians to support each other and the Coca-Cola Company's values and goals, and to achieve balance by integrating their Christian faith at work." This is accomplished through weekly prayer meetings and Bible studies and by providing help to those in need. After a hurricane in Jamaica, the Coca-Cola Christian Fellowship gathered over 90 boxes of clothing to send to the island country, and the company paid for the freight to ship them.

The Toyota Christian Fellowship, located in two major plants in Kentucky, started in 2003. A group at Continental Airlines began in 1996 with two people who began to meet for prayer over lunch. Today, the group has more than 450 members. Similar groups have been established at AOL, American Airlines, Intel, Texas Instruments and Sears. The Christian fellowship at Sears even has its own choir and has produced a professionally recorded CD, which was underwritten by the company.

One notable feature of this movement in major companies is that there tends to be more unity among believers in the workplace than in local churches. Divisive denominational issues pale in comparison to the common challenge the employees of these companies face in living out their faith at work.

The Movement in Academia

Today, nearly 100 Christian colleges offer business programs that are designed to teach the next generation what it means to lead and manage a business from a biblical perspective. Moreover, the Christian Business Faculty Association has grown from its humble beginnings in 1980 to boast more than 400 members and its own academic journal, the *Journal of Biblical Integration in Business*. But the academic movement is not limited just to Christian schools. InterVarsity Christian Fellowship has launched or supported Christian fellowships in dozens of the best secular business schools in the world, including Harvard, Duke, Columbia, Dartmouth, MIT, Michigan, Northwestern, Chicago, Wharton, Virginia, Yale and the London School of Business.

The Movement in Publishing

Whenever there is a move of God, people write about it, and the Faith at Work movement is no exception. Pete Hammond, author of the *Marketplace Annotated Bibliography,* states that by 2000 there were approximately 350 titles published about the faith-workplace connection, with the first books published in the 1930s. By early 2005, there were over 2000 titles by Christians about the faith-workplace connection, some focusing on leadership and management and other speaking to issues faced by all Christian workers. Since that time this trend has only increased, with more and more publishers entering this category.

In recent years, magazines for Christians who want to understand how to live their faith at work have been launched. Among them are *Life@Work, The Christian Businessman* (both now out of publication), *Business Reform* and the *Regent Business Review*. In addition, a plethora of websites and e-mail newsletters have been spawned, adding more fuel to the movement.

The Movement in Ministries

The International Coalition of Workplace Ministries (ICWM), Scruples.net, and the Coalition for Ministry in Daily Life are three ministries that all serve the Faith at Work movement and track its growth. In 2004, Yale University established the Yale Center for Faith and Culture, which sponsors ongoing programs, fixed-term projects and short-term initiatives dedicated to understanding and revitalizing the ways in which religious commitments interact with culture and shape people's lives.

Fourteen years ago, I could identify only 25 to 50 national or international non-profit workplace ministries; today there are more than 900. In 2004, an International Faith and Work Directory featured more than 1,400 listings of ministries, businesses and churches that have a focus on integrating faith and work.

Among these proliferating ministries, some of the larger ones are the Christian Business Men's Committee, the International Christian Chamber of Commerce, Businessmen's Fellowship International, Fellowship of Companies for Christ International, the C12 Group and the Christian Management Association (CMA). Indicative of the experience of many of these ministries, growth in CMA has accelerated from a handful of members in 1976 to today over 3,500 CEOs, business owners, middle managers, pastors and church administrators representing more than 1,500 organizations, businesses and churches.

Whereas these larger ministries seek to provide a full-service training and fellowship experience to members, many other Faith at Work ministries are primarily event driven, usually offering prayer breakfasts, a speaker series or Bible studies. A typical representative is Bill Leonard, a real estate executive in Atlanta, who decided to reach out to the hi-tech community by sponsoring a once-a-year "High Tech Prayer Breakfast." Every October, leaders in the high-tech community come to hear an inspirational talk that usually includes a salvation message integrated into it. Table sponsors bring business associates as a means of introducing seekers to Christ. In 2004, more than 1,500 people attended the event. The High Tech Prayer Breakfast has spawned other such events in the real estate and financial services industries.

The Movement in the Local Church

Several years ago, George Barna and Mark Hatch made the assessment that "workplace ministry will be one of the core future innovations in church ministry."[6] Though this is now beginning to be realized, Doug Sherman, co-author of *Your Work Matters to God,* cautions that the local church has been slow to embrace this message. He states, "Our surveys reveal that 90 to 97 percent of Christians have never been trained to apply biblical faith to their work life."[7]

I can vouch for those statistics. Whenever I ask a church group if they have been intentionally trained to apply biblical faith in the context of their work life, I rarely get more than a few raised hands. However, there are some positive signs that this might be changing. Dr. Bill Hamon is president of Christian International Business Network (CIBN), a division of Christian International, which is a church-based ministry with a goal of raising up a "company of prophetic apostolic business people," according to the ministry's vision statement. CIBN has one of the most developed networks for church-based workplace ministries in the United States, as well as abroad.

Doug Spada's California-based His Church at Work ministry is one of the newest pioneering efforts to equip the local church to focus on faith at work issues. Spada's ministry does this by creating the infrastructure for a sustainable work-life ministry. His ultimate vision is that churches will send out members to minister in the workplace, just as missionaries are sent out to foreign lands. "We help people launch full-blown ministries within their church," Spada explains. "This isn't, 'Hey, let's meet for breakfast.' This is more of an embedded ministry which makes it part of the DNA of the local church." Beyond that vision, Spada says there's a broader reason for the local church to be creating work-life ministries. "Spiritual renewal movements, particularly in Western culture, are almost always birthed and driven by all segments of a working society, not just the leaders."

Karen Jones, director of workplace ministry at Southeast Christian Church in Louisville, Kentucky, agrees. "I believe it is a move of God. I believe it's cutting edge—the next mission field." Southeast Christian

Church launched its workplace ministry two years ago based on Spada's model, and Jones says her initial goal is to involve at least half of the church's 20,000 members. "Statistics say that each person has a sphere of influence of about 25," she comments. "So we could be influencing 250,000 people a week very quickly if people understood that their workplace was a mission field." The impact in the community could be tremendous.

The 5,000-member Wooddale Church in Eden Prairie, Minnesota, is another church that has adopted Spada's process. Geoff Bohleen, outreach pastor for Wooddale, says workplace ministry allows his church to reach out to the people that they would never reach otherwise. "There's no way our pastoral staff is going to get into all those offices—but our people are already there," he explains. "Our pastoral staff is limited in terms of the connections, the relationships and the friendships we can have with people who need Christ. However, we've got 'Wooddalers' all over the place."

A Catalyst for Revival

In his book *The Spirit of the Disciplines: Understanding How God Changes Lives,* Dallas Willard notes, "There is truly no division between sacred and secular except what we have created. And that is why the division of the legitimate roles and functions of human life into the sacred and secular does incalculable damage to our individual lives and the cause of Christ. Holy people must stop going into 'church work' as their natural course of action and take up holy orders in farming, industry, law, education, banking, and journalism with the same zeal previously given to evangelism or to pastoral and missionary work."[8]

That message is getting through as the Faith at Work movement sweeps across the land, and the potential is great for it to effect genuine revival across the culture. Dr. Peter Wagner, noted church growth expert and former professor at Fuller Theological Seminary, also foresees this revival. In *The Faith@Work Movement,* Dr. Wagner notes, "I believe the workplace movement has the potential to impact society as much as the

Reformation did. I have read 84 books on this movement and have 54 pages of handwritten notes. It is what the Spirit is saying to the churches today."[9]

Below is a list of what I believe we can expect to see in the next five years as a result of God's move among believers in the workplace:

- intentional training along with practical application in the local church to help men and women understand that their work is a ministry, along with practical application
- churches that equip and support Christians in their workplace callings
- a movement similar to Promise Keepers, with major events around the Faith at Work theme
- the integration of the Faith at Work message into the focus of the men's movement
- a more proactive acceptance of Faith at Work issues on the part of corporations
- prayer making more of an impact in the workplace
- the transformation of cities, as those in authority become more active and passionate about their faith where they work
- a greater expression of faith in government agencies, the entertainment industry, educational institutions and corporate workplaces
- a greater number of people coming to Christ as major ministries embrace this move of God and integrate it into their operations
- an increased number of miracles in the marketplace because of Christians who are willing to move into arenas that the religious leaders have believed were taboo
- influential roles for pastors, who, although often last to embrace the movement, will find it to be the breakthrough they have been seeking

In other words, there is a revival coming; a revival that is returning us to our roots to understand what the Early Church understood—that work is a holy calling in which God moves to transform lives, cities and nations.

Indeed, we live in historic times. Using our collective influence in companies, ministries, colleges, the media and the local church, God has suddenly and providentially begun reaching the 9 to 5 Window. Let us not miss our opportunity to be part of this movement.

How About You?

1. Can you see the move of God in your workplace? Cite three areas where you have seen the activity of God in the workplace in recent years.
2. List three ways you might be able to start making a positive Christian impact in your workplace.

PART II:

BRINGING GOD'S POWER INTO YOUR WORKPLACE

CHAPTER 8

HEARING THE VOICE OF GOD—EVEN ON THE JOB

I am the good shepherd; I know my sheep and my sheep know me . . .
My sheep listen to my voice; I know them, and they follow me.

JOHN 10:14,27

Tom Fox is a successful financial investment manager who heads up a workplace ministry in the Twin Cities, Minnesota, area. He used to be troubled when he heard Christians say, "The Lord told me . . . " He certainly had never heard God speak to him like that. *What is different about those people and me?* he wondered. In the book of John, he had read that Jesus had said that His sheep hear His voice, but he didn't understand how they could do that. His pursuit to answer that question began his quest to discover how to hear God's voice himself.

Today, Tom realizes that God does speak and that we, as His children, can hear His voice. He has discovered how to hear God's words of guidance in his daily life, which includes the day-to-day operations of his business, and he is teaching others how to hear God's voice as well.

A friend of mine told me a story about an experience he had in Israel that demonstrates how sheep know their shepherd's voice. He and his wife were visiting some of the famous biblical sites when they saw a group of shepherds and their flocks. They watched as three different shepherds put their sheep in the same pen for the night, and they wondered how in the world the shepherds would separate their sheep the next day, since none of them had any identifying marks on them.

My friend got up early the next morning to watch the shepherds gather their sheep. The first shepherd went over to the pen and called out to his sheep. One by one, his sheep (and only his sheep) filed out to follow him. The same thing happened with the other two shepherds. My friend said it was amazing to watch how only the shepherd's sheep followed him while the others remained in the pen—and all because they recognized his voice. What a picture of Jesus' words spoken centuries earlier.

Developing Intimacy With God

If Jesus is the good Shepherd and His sheep know His voice, how can we learn to hear Him speak? The answer is to develop intimacy with God first, so that our hearts are familiar enough with Him to be able to recognize His voice.

Ken Gire, in his book *The Divine Embrace,* describes the intimacy Jesus had with the disciples:

Before Jesus called the disciples to ministry, He called them to intimacy. Following came first; fishing came later. Before he called them to represent him, he called them to *be* with him. Jesus appointed the twelve that they might be *with* him and that he might send them out to preach and to have authority over demons (see Mark 3:14-15). Before he sent them out he drew them close. He went out with them publicly so they could hear him teach and see him heal the sick and cast out demons (see Luke 6:12-19). At times, he withdrew from them privately so they could be with him without distraction (see Luke 9:10). Even as he was leaving the earth he promised he would always be *with* them (see Matthew 28:20). And later, Luke tells us, the credentials by which the disciples were recognized was that of "having been with Jesus" (Acts 4:13).[1]

Developing an intimate relationship with God is vital if we want to experience a fruitful life that is led by His Spirit. Jesus longs to have daily fellowship with each of us because He truly loves us. He will help us fall in love with Him in response to His love.

My wife knows firsthand what it's like to fall in love with God. At the age of 29, Angie was single and worked as an account executive in an advertising agency. Her personal life was filled with struggles. One day, her Christian boss led her in praying the sinner's prayer. When she said "amen," Angie thought, *Whew! Now I know I'm going to heaven and I can get on with the rest of my life.*

At first, she didn't attend church, but eventually she began to do so. It was there she learned that Christianity is a lot more than a ticket to heaven. Reading in Matthew 7:8 that "everyone who asks receives," she prayed and asked God for "a husband or someone to fill the gap." She then saw the words, "Be still and know that I am God," which she felt had been written just for her. She was hungry for more of God, and she spent every available moment reading her Bible and getting to know what God was like.

After a couple of years, the Lord had transformed her life to such a degree that she hardly recognized herself. However, she did not yet have a husband, so she asked God for the second time to send someone to her.

A few days later, she got a note from a friend with "Psalm 27:14" written at the bottom. Sensing that this was an answer to her request for a husband, she ran to her Bible to find out what it said. Much to her dismay, the verse read: "Wait for the Lord, be strong and take heart and wait for the Lord." Angie was disappointed. However, when she mentioned her dismay to a friend at work, she received a response that surprised her. "You are where my wife was before she met me," her friend said. "She realized she needed to fall in love with the Lord before she could love someone else."

Angie pondered that strange comment for days. She realized that she had come to know God as her provider, but that there was quite possibly supposed to be more to the relationship. So she asked the Lord to teach her how to fall in love with Him, though she was not sure He would answer a request that was so personal.

A few days later, a friend called to invite her to go on a women's retreat at the last minute. Through a series of events that were obviously orchestrated by God, Angie found herself at a three-day retreat with a wedding theme based on verses from Hosea 2:16,19-20, which read:

> "In that day," declares the Lord, "you will call me 'my husband'; you will no longer call me 'my master.' . . . I will betroth you to me forever; I will betroth you in righteousness and justice, in love and compassion. I will betroth you in faithfulness, and you will acknowledge the Lord."

That weekend, Angie was "wooed by the Lord." At the end of the three days, she went to the altar and promised Him that she would never again ask for a husband. She told the Lord that she would let Him be her husband.

Over the next few months, Angie says, "Life with Him became so much sweeter than any relationship I'd had with a man." The Lord began to show His love for her in tangible, even romantic, ways, and Angie felt content. In the beginning He had told her to be still and know that He was God. Seven fulfilling years later, He answered her prayer for a husband—me. By that time, she was so happy with her divine Husband that she was concerned about having a flesh-and-blood one; she didn't want to lose her intimacy with God.

Angie claims, "Jesus remains the greatest romance of my life. He has taken a person who was not seeking Him in any way, shape or form and transformed her life in a way that is best described in 1 Peter 1:8: 'Though you have not seen him, you love him; and even though you do not see him now, you believe in him and are filled with an inexpressible and glorious joy.'"

Following the Voice of God

If we are going to experience the reality of intimacy with God, we must do it in our daily work lives. Let me share with you how God led one company to develop intimacy within the context of a working environment.

Julian Watts and Warren Sinclair, who operate an international company called Markets Unlocked in Guildford, England, have learned how important intimacy and the presence of God is to fulfilling His purposes for their business. Even the existence of their company is a testimony of the Lord's loving pursuit, faithful guidance, grace-filled preparations and His plans, which surpass anything Julian and Warren could have thought or imagined.

Julian used to be a partner in the strategy consultancy practice of a global consultancy firm that worked with chief executives of multinational corporations. He gave money to his local church and managed a quiet time with the Lord every couple of weeks when he could fit it into his schedule. In contrast to the high-profile nature of his job, he always kept a low profile on Sundays, usually sitting at the back of the church.

In 1999, the Lord asked Julian if he would be willing to resign his partnership, leave the company and walk out into the unknown. Having spent 15 years single-mindedly achieving his goal to become a strategy consulting partner, Julian was now hearing the Lord's voice saying, "What is more important to you—your career or Me?" He discussed this with his wife, and her brief response was simply, "We've just got to follow the Lord." Julian resigned.

He was now without a job, and he had no idea what to do next. He spent the next few months attempting to discover what the Lord wanted him to do. Eventually, he founded an internet company that specialized in connecting businesses that wanted to buy and sell to each other. He set about building the new company, focusing on all the commercial fundamentals and occasionally praying for God's help to get the task done.

Julian also established a charitable trust in which 10 percent of the company's revenue would be deposited for distribution to Kingdom projects. He felt that God wanted him to pay salaries to other people in the company, but that he and his wife should not draw a salary until the company had started making contributions to the charitable trust. God was calling them to live by faith and to depend totally on Him, an experience that would profoundly change their Christian experience and relationship with the Lord.

The business grew very quickly, riding on the crest of the Internet wave. But the dotcom crash that swiftly followed in the year 2000 was brutal, and the company was all but wiped out. As things were getting worse, the non-Christians in the company left, and the remaining Christian directors started praying together—monthly at first, then, as things continued to worsen, weekly, and finally, as desperation set in, daily!

In the beginning, the directors' prayers just had one focus—the list of things required to save the business. However, the more time they spent with the Lord, the more things began to change. Gradually, the list of urgent prayer requests gave way to simply worshiping God—seeking His face rather than His hand of provision. Now that they had a considerably smaller staff, they set aside a room in their office space for company prayer. Since their corporate communications director, Liz Jones, no longer had much to communicate about, she started spending more and more of her time in the prayer room, worshiping the Lord and praying for the company. The more the directors simply worshiped the Lord, the more they saw Him intervene. Throughout the rest of 2000 and into 2001, time after time, the Lord would provide just what was needed at the eleventh hour.

The directors' daily routines soon began to change. At first, Julian started having his own personal time with the Lord from 5:00 A.M. to 7:00 A.M. each day. Then, from 8:00 A.M. to 9:00 A.M., all the company directors would meet to worship and pray. From 9:00 A.M. to 2:00 P.M. every weekday, Liz would worship and intercede for the company; and every Tuesday from 10:00 A.M. to 12:00 P.M., everyone in the company would meet, along with local pastors and intercessors, to worship and intercede.

Liz was now the trailblazer for the rest of the company. During the hours she spent in the Lord's presence, God started speaking to her about her personal identity as part of the Bride of Christ. The Lord then began to increasingly speak this message of intimacy with Him to other people in the company. They began to dare to believe that He viewed them as part of His beloved Bride, that He was passionately in love with them as believers, and that He had died so that they could commune with Him.

By late 2001, the company had passed through the wilderness of the dotcom crash. In the process, all the commercial aspects of the company had been completely transformed—including its business strategy, organization structure, people, operational processes, location and everything else. Experiencing God's presence is now the heart and driving force of the company. Each workday, the directors' personal and corporate prayer times are characterized by simply worshiping the Lord. After worshiping, the directors ask if anyone is hearing from the Lord. Based on that feedback, they intercede for whatever God has indicated.

Today, the directors see that the Lord is increasingly establishing their company's corporate identity and defining characteristic as their corporate intimacy with Him. Markets Unlocked is now expanding rapidly around the world, with customers in over 80 countries.

How Does God Speak?

As we have already glimpsed in this chapter, God speaks to His children in many ways, primarily through the Bible, an audible voice, a "still, small voice" or thoughts, circumstances, prophetic words, and visions and dreams. Let's examine each of these ways that God speaks to us.

The Bible

The Bible is loaded with principles to guide us in our daily lives and should always be the standard by which we weigh all the other methods of hearing God's voice. Spending time reading the Bible and knowing what it says will keep us from making mistakes as we discover the other ways that God speaks. The Bible is often referred to as the "living" Word of God. As you read your Bible, you can expect God to speak to you directly and personally through the words on the page.

God used the Bible to speak to me when I was still grappling with financial difficulties. I had already felt called to help men and women understand their workplace calling, but I had no idea how it would come to pass, and I certainly had no income to support it. I was in such a hard place that I was unable to pray, so instead of trying to do something in my own strength, I asked Angie to come over and pray with me (we weren't married yet). Angie prayed for me and asked the Lord to give us wisdom.

Within a couple of minutes, she blurted out, "First Thessalonians 5:24!"

"What verse is that?" I asked.

"I have no idea," she replied. "It just popped into my head."

I grabbed my Bible, looked it up and read, "The one who calls you is faithful and he will do it." We laughed. Could God be so personal? Could He care that much? That night, God encouraged me to be at peace with the situation in which I found myself. He never failed me once through the difficult years, and now we have a ministry to those in the workplace. God has brought it about.

An Audible Voice

Scripture records many occurrences when God spoke audibly to His children. God spoke to Moses face to face. When Adam and Eve enjoyed unbroken fellowship in the Garden of Eden, they had a two-way dialogue with God.

My mother tells of her own personal experience in hearing the audible voice of God. She was at a low point in her life after my father was killed. For months, she cried out to God in her grief and anguish. After learning that none of the insurance companies were going to pay, she was about to have a nervous breakdown. But one night while she was weeping, she heard an audible voice say, "Trust me, Lillian." That is all she heard that night and it never happened again, but that one experience has kept her for more than 40 years.

A "Still, Small Voice" or Thoughts

Many people describe "hearing" God speak through a sense of "knowing" that often comes in their thoughts. That's what happened for Angie in the story above, when 1 Thessalonians 5:24 popped into her head.

My good friend Dr. Victor Eagan, an orthodontist and leader of an international marketplace ministry, says, "I have found that God often speaks personally to me when I am not seeking to hear Him. In other words, I don't often hear Him speak when I am having my quiet time. More often it is when I am in my car or in the shower."

My friend Brenda found this to be true one time when she was on a flight. Words came into her mind that said, "There is a woman on the plane who you need to find. I want you to pray for her." Not knowing what to do, she walked down the aisle to see if the Lord would show her the woman, and He did. Stepping out in faith, she approached the woman and said, "Pardon me, this is going to seem strange, but may I pray for you?" Without giving the woman much time to respond, Brenda began praying and found that she was being led to pray for comfort in relation to the woman's husband.

After she had prayed, the woman shared with Brenda that her husband had just died. "Normally, my family would pray with me," she said, "But due to the rush of getting on the plane, they could not. But my mother-in-law told me that someone would pray with me on the plane." The woman was deeply touched and felt as if God had reached down from heaven to let her know that He cared about her.

Another friend, John Wright from England, told me about his conversation with a Muslim man as they walked together in the country. John wanted to share the gospel with him, but knew little about the man's Muslim beliefs. The two men agreed they would each share their religious beliefs with one another. The Muslim went first and dominated the conversation.

As the man spoke, John asked the Holy Spirit how to share his faith with him. Suddenly, a thought came to him. "Do you consider your god to be your father who speaks?" he asked.

"Certainly not," replied the Muslim man.

"That is one of the big differences between your god and my God. I consider my God as my Father who speaks to me personally."

"You cannot prove that," retorted the Muslim man.

John again prayed silently, "Lord, how do I prove this to him?"

A few moments later, two young ladies came walking toward them. As they approached, John spoke to them and made polite conversation. Then he said to one woman, "I believe you are a nurse, is that correct?"

Startled, she asked, "How would you know that? I have never met you before."

He replied, "I asked my Father and He told me." The Holy Spirit had impressed the word "nurse" on his mind. The Muslim man had his proof.

Circumstances

God will often speak to us through our circumstances. It is easy to miss God speaking to us in this way because we are not looking for His special touches throughout our ordinary days.

Before we were married, Angie had an experience of divine direction that developed circumstantially. She was desperate to find a place to live after moving to St. Simons Island, Georgia, to work for a non-profit ministry. She had taken a huge cut in pay to work there and finding a place she could afford had proven to be impossible. Here's her story:

> I knew God had a place for me. One day as I was talking to Him about it, I said, "if only you could show me where it is." I pictured in my head a neon sign lit up against a nighttime sky that said "here it is" with an arrow pointing to the place where I was supposed to live. Of course, I knew that was silly, but I wished God would give me that kind of sign.
>
> With only a few days left in the condo the ministry had let me live in, I went to look at the only house in the area that I could afford to live in. The only problem was that it had huge gaping holes in the walls and was practically falling apart. (I later learned that it had been condemned!) The owner was not willing to do anything to fix it up, but it was the only option I had at that point. I went to look at the house one final time, and as I prayed I felt no sense of peace. So I walked out thinking, *OK, God, you must have something else.*
>
> As I was driving away, I passed by a little side street that had a *huge* orange sign in the window that said "For Rent." The sign

was at least five feet wide and four feet tall. I slammed on the brakes, backed up and pulled in the driveway. The owner just happened to be inside and showed me around the most beautiful little beach cottage I had ever seen—and it was only 80 steps from the beach! I loved it, but I knew there was no way I could afford it. The owner gave me his card and told me to call him if I changed my mind.

My next stop was a little gift shop in the village. A sales clerk asked me if I needed help finding anything and I said, "I need a place to live." Her response blew me away. "Well you've come to the right place. This is a place where miracles happen." The store owner assured me that she would do everything to help me and told me about how she had found a place for her friend who had just moved there. At that moment, her friend walked in the store and she introduced us. The next thing I knew, I was having lunch with the store owner's friend.

To make a long story short, I ended up living in the little cottage with the lady I met in the store, and we are still friends today, 10 years later. God gave me the "neon sign" I was looking for and a wonderful roommate so that I could afford it. God demonstrated His love and care for me through some amazing circumstances. That taught me to always be on the lookout for Him in the "everyday" things.

Prophetic Words

I came from a church background that did not expose me to ministry that involved prophecy or words of knowledge. However, God has brought people into my life who clearly operate in these gifts, and I have come to see them as valuable tools to affirm Christians in their faith and calling.

The word "prophecy" comes from the Greek word *propheteia*, which means, "the speaking forth of the mind and counsel of God." A further explanation in *Vines Dictionary* states:

Though much of old testament prophecy was purely predictive, prophecy is not necessarily, nor even primarily, fore-telling. It is the declaration of that which cannot be known by natural means, it is the forth-telling of the will of God, whether with reference to the past, the present, or the future. Scripture encourages us to eagerly desire spiritual gifts, especially the gift of prophecy (1 Cor. 14:1); and to not treat prophecies with contempt, but to test everything and hold on to the good (1 Thess. 5:20-21).[2]

These are God's methods of communication to us through others. Such communication from God does not have to be presented using terms such as "prophecy"; it may come in a simple conversation with another person, who might say something that strikes a chord in your spirit, perhaps confirming something you heard from someone else. Be alert to these types of situations. God is using them to communicate important information to you. Let me give you a couple of personal examples.

When Angie and I met for the first time, she told me she was called to the mission field. The moment she said that, I heard in my inner spirit, *She is called to the mission field, but it is not what she thinks*. I did not mention this to her. However, when we were together the following week, she asked if I would pray for her. She was about to sell all of her belongings to go to the mission field, but was unsure where she was to go. That's when I told her, "You're called to the mission field, but it's not what you think." She actually got upset with me because she thought I was trying to date her and disrupt her calling. But a few days later, she called to say that whenever she felt God giving her direction, it was never what she thought it was.

Nine months later, we were married. One night, as she was lying in bed, this thought came to her mind: *You thought your mission field was somewhere overseas when it is actually six inches away, beside you*. Angie has worked alongside me in our ministry since we were married. Now she realizes that she is indeed called to the mission field, but it definitely is not what she thought it would be.

I was strongly encouraged by prophetic words around this same time in my own life. One came as an e-mail from a friend in another state, which read:

I believe that God is saying that the worst is over for you and that you need not fear any repeat of the pain of the past. You are not a second-rate son, as the enemy of your soul will try to tell you. Lift up your eyes and see your Father smiling at you. From now on, you will work with God, rather than just for Him. He will show you the plan and the steps. You have learned to wait for His voice. There is a latter rain for your life. It will refresh you and cause you to forget the dryness of the past. Even now, the clouds are forming. There will be new crops, new fields, new harvests, new plantings, new partners in your life.

This was echoed and confirmed when, at a conference, a man named Bradley Stuart came forward with a word of prophecy for someone in the audience. The minute he read his words I knew they were for me. Here is the message the Lord gave him:

The past few years have been times of deep preparation where I have allowed you and your business to be torn and smitten. But this is the season where I want to start to restore and heal you. However, right now, as you are about to be restored, it is a time when I want you to allow me to show you what I have been teaching you. The seed is about to spring forth, so simply wait and rest in me. I am in control, I am working on the seed and it shall come forth as I send the gentle rains.

Among other things, the first message was also another confirmation to me about Angie, whom I would marry eight months later, and who represented a new planting and new partner in my life.

Visions and Dreams

The Bible is full of examples of God speaking to people through visions and dreams. God can use dreams to give us specific direction or revelation about something in our lives.

In Acts 10, a man named Cornelius had a life-changing vision one day at about three in the afternoon. He distinctly saw an angel of God, who came to him and said, "Cornelius!" The angel instructed him to send some men to get a man named Peter in another town. The following day, God gave Peter a vision in which He instructed him to go with some men to the house of Cornelius. The obedient responses of both men to the visions God gave them resulted in immediate conversions and the beginning of the spread of the gospel to the non-Jewish world.

God still speaks through visions and dreams. Our five-year-old nephew came over for a sleepover. When he awoke the next morning, he told Angie about a dream he had had the night before in which a bulldozer came down our driveway and knocked our house down. Angie was thrilled! Our home was literally falling apart. For three years she had had to wash her hair in water heated on the stove because otherwise the water turned her hair green. Our home had been for sale as commercial property and we were waiting for a contract to go through. We both sensed this was God's way of telling us it would sell. Six months later, the deal closed and we became debt-free—and the house was bulldozed a few months later! Angie's nephew had no idea that any of this was in the works.

The Difference Between Religion and Relationship

In Psalm 32:8, God speaks through the psalmist to tell us that He indeed will give us direction and instruction: "I will instruct you and teach you in the way you should go; I will counsel you and watch over you." In the Church today, we often think the only way God speaks is through the Bible. (Someone once said, "You would think some churches think the Trinity is more like the Father, Son and *Holy Scriptures*.") There is such a focus on the Word of God to the exclusion of the other ways God speaks that it is no wonder we do not find out what God wants us to do.

Because so many of us do not know how to listen for God's voice, we're not able to hear Him in our places of employment. In order to hear, we must believe and take the time to listen. We must depend not only on our logical reasoning, but also leave room for the spontaneity of the Holy Spirit in our lives.

The difference between hearing God's voice and not hearing it is the difference between having a relationship with God and just having a religion. God wants to have an intimate relationship with you to enable you to hear His voice speaking to you. Ask Him to give you sensitive ears to hear and the courage to obey His voice.

How About You?

1. Intimacy is developed by spending time with the person you want to be close to. List some ways you can develop a greater level of intimacy with Jesus.

2. When was the last time you sensed that God was speaking to you? List some ways you can begin today to better listen for the voice of God in your life.

CHAPTER 9

INTERCESSORY PRAYER IN THE WORKPLACE

Epaphras, who Paul states to the Colossians "is one of you and a servant of Christ Jesus. . . . He is always wrestling in prayer for you, that you may stand firm in all the will of God, mature and fully assured."

COLOSSIANS 4:12

Because we've been entrenched in the "secular versus sacred" model for so long, it can be difficult for us to view our work as a ministry and workplace believers as missionaries in the 9 to 5 Window. However, God tells us clearly that we are to glorify God in all that we do (see Col. 3:17,24). One way we can do this is through intercessory prayer, which can be characterized as an intense type of prayer for others (see Eph. 6:18; Col. 4:12), the priestly calling of all believers (see 1 Pet. 2:5; Exod. 19:6) and the Holy Spirit praying in us (see Rom. 8:26-27). Having people pray for us to fulfill our purpose and calling in our workplaces is consistent with the will of God for every individual.

Imagine if all corporations had a director of corporate intercession as a paid position. I am pleased to tell you that in at least one case, this is already happening. Darlene Maisano is a full-time intercessor for the marketplace and a paid intercessor for several businesses. She is paid as a consultant would be paid. She sits in business meetings, quietly praying and "listening." She has authored the only resource I know of on the subject, *Breaking Open the Doors of Success Through Marketplace Intercession*. Here are her thoughts on the importance of workplace intercession:

> Through the birthing and establishing of the Church, nothing has ever been accomplished on earth without prayer and intercession. And with the restoration of the workplace, intercession is a key to bridging the gap, making a way and nullifying the shortage of laborers in the Kingdom.
>
> Whereas we once thought of those involved in politics, economics, religion, and the military as the ones controlling the earth, today we recognize the enormous influence wielded by those in the workplace.
>
> As a workplace intercessor for numerous national and international businesses, I have experienced the importance of interceding on their behalf. Favor, wisdom, financial gain and well-being have been manifested and evident in peoples' lives and businesses. I am also seeing a growing number of workplace intercessors stepping up to the plate saying, "That's my calling."[1]

While the idea of a workplace intercessor may be a new concept for us, we need to remember the examples we find in the New Testament of believers praying for one another. One such example is Epaphras, who Paul states to the Colossians "is one of you and a servant of Christ Jesus. . . . He is always wrestling in prayer for you, that you may stand firm in all the will of God, mature and fully assured" (Col. 4:12).

Let me give you a modern example of what I am describing as intercessory prayer in the workplace.

Intercessory Prayer in an Optical Company

Colin Ferreira is a friend, a board member for our ministry and an owner of an optical business in Trinidad. I first met Colin in 2001 when he invited me to speak at a Caribbean workplace conference that he was organizing. I have watched Colin develop into a Kingdom business leader whose vision is to see his nation transformed.

For many years, Colin considered his business to be a Kingdom business as well as his primary calling to ministry, even though he had also been in church leadership. At his workplace, he would have weekly prayer meetings and exercise prayer in business meetings whenever he felt the need. For eight years, he led his management staff in a weekly study of the book of Proverbs from a business perspective. The biblical principles they discussed together caused them to change the way they operated the business.

Eighteen years ago, Colin and his management staff made a decision to use a minimum of 10 percent of their profits (before tax) for building the kingdom of God. God blessed their business greatly, and they have been able to support many ministries and provide significant leadership and administrative support to some of those organizations. However, through a series of struggles common to most businesses (made worse due to apparent spiritual opposition), Colin began to recognize the need for more prayer coverage. One of the organizations for which he had been supplying financial and leadership support maintained a House of Prayer. Colin asked the minister who headed the organization to intercede for him and his company on an ongoing basis, and she gladly agreed.

The two met periodically to discuss prayer needs and critical issues developing within the organization, which the minister then addressed discreetly in her intercessory group meetings. Often, this woman would recognize specific problems during these prayer meetings and know how to pray for them effectively. This became the first step to Colin developing intercessory prayer within his own company. In his words:

God continued to nudge me to go a step further. Business being as dynamic as it is, there is constant need for prayer on the spot and in meetings. We also realized that we needed to take a more proactive approach to taking and maintaining authority over the business in the spirit realm at every location. I felt that God was saying that we were to have someone fulltime on staff. The question was, How do we have someone on our payroll without raising a heap of questions and criticisms from our non-Christian employees?

We went before the Lord with that question and He gave us an answer. We established a new position called the Employee Assistance Officer/Intercessor. To our 120 employees, her function is that of an Employee Assistance Officer, and her job is to identify ways we can provide tangible and practical assistance to employees with problems. Her role fulfills a need that exists and that was a genuine concern of our company, as we desire employees to function at their best.

She visits our six locations periodically to connect with employees and identify those with problems. These problems could be marital, parenting, housing, financial or medical, to name a few. Her role is to provide counsel, guidance, direction and other tangible forms of assistance with careful assessment of each situation.

In order to develop this area further, Colin decided to get some training for both his intercessor and himself at Christian International in Florida, an organization that is experienced in developing believers' ability to receive prophetic input from God. Colin strongly believes that a Christian CEO should be able to hear the voice of God for himself and not be heavily dependent on someone else's communication with God. He also believes that, in an effort to stop dividing things into "secular" or "spiritual," such training should be just as important as a management training seminar, if not more so. The training proved to be very enlightening, practical and necessary for both of them.

Colin states that his Employee Assistance Officer now develops her prayer strategies in the following way:

On her location visits, besides identifying employee problems, she tries to identify the spiritual problems in each specific location.

These vary from place to place and may even involve witchcraft as evidenced by paraphernalia known to specific cults. A team of intercessors (including a company director) revisits the location outside of working hours to pray specifically for the needs and situation of that location. Every week, a different location is visited.

Our intercessor is also involved in the employee weekly prayer meeting and, particularly, the senior management prayer meeting, where sensitive and confidential situations are addressed. From time to time as we are praying, she will receive a vision or word from the Lord that will either confirm something or provide more clarity or direction that later proves to be on target. She is also on call throughout the day to pray as situations arise.

We are still learning from the Lord in this area of intercession in our business. I do not believe that there is a set formula for the use of intercessors in a business organization as each situation has its uniqueness. However, I do believe that it is a necessary and vital function for any Kingdom organization in these times.

My First Encounter with an Intercessor

In June of 1996, Christian Financial Concepts (now Crown Ministries), a ministry led by Larry Burkett, published my testimony in their monthly newsletter. Shortly after the article appeared, a call came into our office from a woman named Jan. She mentioned that she had a ministry of intercessory prayer and said she was calling because she sensed the Lord had told her to do so. A mentor and I had just been discussing the need for intercessors to undergird the work we were beginning, but I did not learn until later what that really meant.

Jan came to our office a few days later and met with Sue, my mentor's wife, who was using some of my office space. Sue was a real prayer warrior herself, often awaking in the middle of the night to pray for those God put on her heart. The two women soon began praying together. After a while, Jan tentatively revealed to Sue that she felt led to pray for three men. When she prayed for the third man, she described seeing a boy between the ages of 12 and 14 who had played basketball, experienced a major crisis in his life, and had grown up with a burden of insecurity that had plagued him most of his life. She prayed for him and asked Sue if she knew who this man might be. There was no doubt that this was me—my dad had died when I was 14, I had played basketball and I was then in the process of being freed from a stronghold of insecurity and fear. The other two men turned out to be Sue's husband and my last employee from the advertising agency.

When I heard about this, I was shocked. I thought, *Who is this "seer" who has come into my office?* A few days later, Jan and I met at a restaurant. This was my first introduction to a prayer intercessor. We prayed together, and at the conclusion of our prayer time, Jan said the Lord showed her that I would be speaking to a lot of men and women in large settings. Tears came to my eyes, because this confirmed a dream in which I had been speaking to a large group of people. Now, almost 10 years later, God has taken me to 14 different countries, where He has allowed me to speak about what He is doing in the workplace and in my personal life. Jan, as she continues to pray, has become a key partner in this ministry.

The Application of Intercessory Prayer in the Workplace

I have found the following process to be the best application of intercessory prayer as I have begun to implement it in my organization. First, I personally pray and consult with my wife on key issues. Next, I ask my prayer team to pray over specific issues and ask for their input as they hear from God. We weigh the feedback from the prayer team and make strategic decisions based on what we believe God is saying to us. We do not believe it is the role of intercessors to dictate strategic action but to confirm direction and make us aware of any "spiritual minefields." Here's a specific example of what I'm talking about.

A few years ago, I was about to meet with some partners on a ministry venture. For months I had been troubled about the foundational direction this venture was taking. However, I had not been able to clearly discern whether it was something that God wanted me to address. I did not share the specifics with Jan but simply asked her to pray about something that I was concerned about. The next morning, Jan sent me an e-mail that said God seemed to impress her to encourage me to boldly address anything that was on my heart, especially anything that was "foundational." She actually used those words. This was confirmation for me to know that what I was sensing was from God, and it gave me the boldness to address my concern. It resulted in me leaving the partnership.

I currently have three types of intercessory prayer relationships:

1. *Pray-ers*. Pray-ers tend to pray for shorter periods of time and often over lists of things for others. I have over 1,000 people who have volunteered to pray for Angie and our ministry. I send out periodic notices to these volunteers about the work we are doing and request prayer for specific things. They rarely report back what they hear to me, as they are not accustomed to "listening" on my behalf.
2. *Intercessors*. I distinguish a difference between one who prays and one who intercedes. The intercessors I have enter into an extended time of prayer on my behalf. They often report back to me on the things they are hearing from the Lord.
3. *Inner Circle Intercessors*. Only one or two people make up my inner circle intercessors. They know my family and me well and often travel with me or participate in key events with our ministry.

So how do you find intercessors and begin working with them? First, ask God to identify them to you. Then ask your pastor for the names of intercessors in the church who might be willing to intercede on your behalf. Once who have found people to be your intercessors, determine your expectations of one another before you begin working together. You may even want to write these expectations out and discuss them together. Finally, it is important to proceed slowly in the relationship to determine if this is something both you and the other parties are comfortable in pursuing.

Compensating Intercessors?

The idea of compensating intercessors by paying them for their time is something that is still in its developmental stage and may represent a new and unusual concept to us. However, we need to move past the roadblock of thinking that it's inappropriate to pay people to pray and realize that those who are spending time praying for a business need to be compensated in the same manner as any other person who is working on its behalf.

The models for employing and compensating intercessors are varied depending on the circumstance, the people involved and the skill and ability of the intercessor. Here are a few examples of some of these models:

- *Employee of the Company.* One company I know has several intercessors who work as regular paid employees. They are there to do a specific job, but they also volunteer their time to pray for the needs of the company.
- *Paid Intercessor.* A company may also hire a person whose primary role is to pray and intercede on its behalf. This individual may become a chaplain to the business as part of this role.
- *Off-site Intercessor Consultant.* An off-site intercessor consultant may work exclusively for one company or for several different companies. He or she might simply be on call to pray for the needs of a particular business and agree to report back to that company on what he or she is hearing. Sometimes this individual's compensation is structured; other times it is provided through periodic love offerings from the company that hires him or her.

It is important to remember that anything can be knocked off track when we get out of balance. Satan desires to get in the mix in any area that does not have proper biblical foundations. Here are just a few things to keep in mind when incorporating intercessors into your work life or business:

- Intercessors should not be viewed as a crystal ball to determine direction. It is the responsibility of leaders to seek God for themselves.
- If an intercessor tells you to take a particular course of action, beware. This is not their role. They are in your life to confirm what you already feel God has spoken to you.
- Avoid making a decision based on one intercessor's input. Gain agreement through more than one source, such as the Bible, circumstances or prayer.
- Try to have a mix of male and female on your intercessory team.
- *You are responsible for the final decision.* You should have a peace about your decision and a willingness to commit it to the Lord should it not fit your rationale all the time. Sometimes it comes down to obedience.
- Know that implementing intercessory prayer into your work or business life requires work and additional time. It takes time to seek the Lord, communicate with others and wait on feedback.

God Is Raising Up Intercessors in the Workplace

What can we expect in the future? In May of 2004, I spoke in Port Elizabeth, South Africa, to a group of city intercessors and workplace leaders representing every church in the city. I told them that if we are going to impact our workplaces, cities and nations, an army of intercessors must be raised up. I stated that God is raising up these intercessors for the workplace today and pledged my support for the raising up of a global network of intercessors that would begin to intercede for the seven major areas that shape society: government, family, arts, religion, education, business and the media.

The intercessors were excited to hear personal examples and teaching on intercession in the marketplace. The leader of the intercessory teams asked all of the workplace leaders to come forward and stand in a circle. They wanted to pray for each of the workplace leaders. It was a prophetic picture of the future—intercessors joining hands with workplace leaders to influence their workplaces, cities and nations. I believe we will see more and more workplace believers desire to have intercessors involved in their work-life call.

In this chapter, I have mostly addressed this topic to leaders of organizations who may want to incorporate intercessory prayer into their organizations. However, intercessory prayer is needed at every level of any organization. Regardless of whether or not you hold a management level position, I want to encourage you to apply the material in this chapter to whatever position you find yourself in. If you are called to great levels of intercession, begin to pray about who you are to intercede for. Just as God is calling forth business leaders to incorporate intercession into their leadership methods, so too is God raising up intercessors for the marketplace. God will lead you to partner with those leaders He has assigned for you to serve.

How About You?

1. God has called each of us to be intercessors at some level. Describe the role prayer currently plays in your work life.
2. Describe some ways you can increase the level of prayer in your life and workplace.

RECEIVING ONLY WHAT GOD GIVES YOU

A man can receive only what is given him from heaven.

JOHN 3:27

John the Baptist was in the business of bringing sinners to the place of repentance by baptizing them and teaching them about the coming Messiah. Over time, he had developed quite a customer base of disciples. Yet when the promised Messiah showed up—the fulfillment of John's business plan—true to form, his coworkers (or disciples) went to John to complain that the one he had testified about was stealing all of his customers. "Rabbi," they said, "that man who was with you on the other side of the Jordan . . . well, he is baptizing, and everyone is going to him" (John 3:26). John's response to his disciples is the point of this chapter: "A man can receive only what is given him from heaven" (John 3:27).

John understood a very important concept. The things that are worth having must be received through obedience to God, not through our own striving and manipulation of outcomes.

A story is told about F. B. Meyer, the great Bible teacher and pastor who lived a century ago. He was pastoring a church when he began to notice that attendance was dropping. This continued until he finally asked some members of his congregation one Sunday morning why they thought this was happening. A member suggested, "It is because of the new church down the road. The young preacher has everyone talking and many are going to hear him speak." The young preacher's name was Charles Spurgeon. Meyer, rather than seeking to discourage this development, exhorted his entire congregation to join him and go participate in seeing this "move of God," as he described it to them. "If this be happening, then God must be at work."[1] Meyer, like John the Baptist, understood the principle of receiving from God and was not threatened by the new competition in town. Instead, he joined it.

The idea of receiving only what God gives you may be a new a concept to you. I had never heard any teaching on it until a friend challenged me about a large piece of real estate I had acquired. He said, "God never gave you that property. You will not keep it. You acquired it out of sweat and toil, not from obedience." I was offended and I thought he was crazy, but he was right—I lost the property, and more.

Each of us must discern what comes from the hand of God rather than our own natural ability. In our workplace, we can rely upon our own abilities and manipulate, sweat and toil our way to profit, or we can trust in God and perform our hard work in obedience to our calling. Knowing the difference between these two concepts is a sign of integrity before God and can only be discerned through intimacy with Him. God receives glory when we receive what He wants us to receive.

Jesus knew what He was to receive. He had the power to have anything He wanted on Earth, yet He modeled this principle by receiving only what His Father wanted Him to receive. God's will for Jesus was to live in a family of common people rather than in a royal palace. Jesus was so sure of His Father's will that He was able to refuse Satan's tempting offer of fame, power and wealth. He understood the vocation He was to have, His standard of living and the death He was to encounter.

Jesus knew why He came to Earth and what He was to receive while on Earth. The people wanted to make Him an earthly king, but He knew that this was not why He came. "Jesus, knowing that they intended to come and make him king by force, withdrew again to a mountain by himself" (John 6:15). Jesus operated from a place that looked like weakness. However, in reality, when we allow God to choose for us and depend upon Him to give us what is best, we operate from a place of strength.

Abraham knew how to trust God to choose for him. When he and Lot determined that the land would not support both of their families, he allowed Lot to choose the land where he wanted to move. Though Abraham could have exercised his authority and seniority, he took the weaker position and allowed Lot to choose the better-looking piece of land. By allowing God to choose for him, Abraham proved his faith and received far more than what he would have had if he had chosen for himself. Abraham modeled the ultimate way to dissolve a partnership—let the other person choose. For in allowing Lot to choose (which was the same as allowing God to choose for him), Abraham not only got the land that Lot didn't want, but also God gave him all the land as far as his eyes could see.

Oswald Chambers learned the distinction between striving to receive from God and letting God choose for us. In his book *My Utmost for His Highest*, he writes,

> God sometimes allows you to get into a place of testing where your own welfare would be the right and proper thing to consider if you were not living a life of faith; but if you are, you will joyfully waive your right and leave God to choose for you. This is the discipline by means of which the natural is transformed into the spiritual by obedience to the voice of God.
>
> Whenever "right" is made the guidance in the life, it will blunt the spiritual insight. The great enemy of the life of faith in God is not sin, but the good which is not good enough. The good is always the enemy of the best. It would seem the wisest thing in the world for Abraham to choose and the people around would consider him a fool for not choosing. Many of us do not go on spiritually because we prefer to choose what is right instead of relying on God to choose for us. We have to learn to walk according to the standard which has its eye on God.[2]

A Modern-Day Example

In the late 1980s, I owned a home on a golf course. This house was a sanctuary to me, and I used to enjoy taking walks around the course in the evenings after the golfers had gone home. I willingly gave up this property in the divorce settlement, even though it was very difficult, because I knew that the Lord was telling me to do so.

Some time later, when Angie and I were looking for a new home, we saw a house for sale on this same golf course where I used to live. We knocked on the door to see if we could take a look at it, and much to our surprise, the owner let us in to check it out. We loved the house, even though the price was a little more than what we wanted to pay. I really felt this was God's house for us and I told Angie that, but she told me that she did not have a peace about the house, though she could not explain why.

I was sure her peace would come. A few weeks later the owner dropped the price by $20,000. My peace was getting better and better! I knew this was our house. I wanted it so badly. It had the greatest view on the entire course. Yet when I asked Angie about it, she said that she still had no peace. However, I was so convinced that it would come that I decided to put a contract on the house. At that point, Angie asked if she could present our dilemma to our marriage accountability group to get their feedback, and I agreed. We each presented our viewpoints to the group and put it to a vote. To my surprise, they voted 100 percent in Angie's favor. I was devastated and dropped the contract.

Strangely, I got a call the following week from the owner of the golf course, who was a personal friend. He asked me if I was still interested in a home on the golf course. Apparently, a woman who just lost her husband was ready to sell. I cynically thought to myself, *If Angie didn't have peace about the other house, why would she have peace about this one?* Nevertheless, I went to see the house.

The home was beautiful. It had a finished basement for our offices and it was perfect for our needs. I knew that Angie would love it, so I brought her back with me the next day. As I had expected, Angie also loved the house, and we decided to make an offer on it. The offer was accepted, and by the end of the transaction we had saved nearly $50,000 in purchasing this house over the other one. We were also able to get to know the widow who sold us the home, and during one of our visits she prayed to receive Christ into her life.

From the experience, I learned that God often returns to us the very thing that we have given up for His sake. He was showing me that He does take us through hard places, but that He also loves to give to His children. The first house was a good house; the second house was *God's* house for us. God received glory from the entire process, and this home has been a great blessing to us. It has allowed us to receive many visitors and has been a place of hospitality and ministry ever since.

Sitting at Jesus' Feet

The biblical story of Ruth and Boaz provides an excellent illustration of the connection between spending time in the presence of God and receiving physical provision.

Ruth and her mother-in-law, Naomi, both widowed and destitute, had returned to Bethlehem, which was Naomi's hometown. As was the custom of the day, Ruth went to gather the leftover grain the harvesters had left behind in the fields. She found herself in a field belonging to Boaz, who was from the clan of her husband's father. After laboring in the fields all day, she had collected about an *ephah* (approximately 22 liters) of barley.

Naomi, realizing that Boaz could provide for them as "kinsman-redeemer," advised Ruth to go to him at the threshing floor, where he would be working and sleeping that night, and to lie at his feet in submission. She did so. As a sign of his blessing, Boaz said to Ruth, "Bring the shawl that is on you and hold it." When she held it out to Boaz, "he measured six ephahs of barley, and laid it on her" (Ruth 3:15, *NKJV*).

Notice that when Ruth worked in the field for a day, she got one ephah of barley. When she laid at her kinsman-redeemer's feet, he gave her six ephahs. The analogy here is that when we, like Ruth, spend time at the feet of Jesus, who is our kinsman-redeemer, He will give us much more than what we could ever produce or gather by our own efforts.

The Temptation to Take Matters Into Our Own Hands

In the process of waiting on God's provision for us, the temptation will be to take matters into our own hands to achieve our desired outcomes. I call this the *horizontal* versus *vertical* method of problem solving. When we seek to solve problems by relying on our own efforts, we are going *horizontal,* or the way of the flesh. However, when we go *vertical,* we take the matter to God, saying, "Lord, I don't understand why I am not getting a breakthrough here, but I know you do. I am going to seek your direction and your timing until I get the breakthrough I need."

There are many examples in the Bible of men and women of faith who took matters into their own hands to get what they wanted. In many cases, these individuals were successful in receiving what they wanted. However, since they did not rely upon God or follow His plan, the Lord brought a penalty or judgment upon them.

Take Moses, for example. In Numbers 20, we read that Moses and the Israelites had been traveling for days without water. The Israelites were angry and quarreled with Moses, saying "Why did you bring us up out of Egypt to this terrible place? It has no grain or figs, grapevines or pomegranates. And there is no water to drink!" (v. 5). So Moses sought the Lord for wisdom about how to handle the situation, and the Lord instructed him, "Take the staff, and . . . *speak to that rock* before their eyes and it will pour out its water" (v. 8, emphasis added). This would show that God was still in control, that Moses was still the leader and that God was their provider.

So Moses took the staff from the Lord's presence, just as he commanded him. He and Aaron gathered the assembly together in front of the rock and Moses said to them, "Listen, you rebels, must we bring you water out of this rock?" Then Moses raised his arm and *struck the rock twice* with his staff. *Water gushed out,* and the community and their livestock drank (vv. 9-11, emphasis added).

Moses' disgust with the people became so great that when it came time to speak to the rock, he angrily addressed the people and instead struck the rock twice. The water came out in spite of Moses' disobedience, but the Lord was not pleased with him. As a consequence, the Lord said to Moses and Aaron, "Because you did not trust in me enough to honor me as holy in the sight of the Israelites, you will not bring this community into the land I give them" (v. 12).

Moses made the mistake many of us make in both our personal lives and in our employment. He used his staff (which, as you remember, represents his vocation and his authority from God) with force to accomplish something. Like Moses, you and I have abilities that allow us to make things happen. We can orchestrate events and even use our abilities to accomplish good things. The problem is that if we do not use our abilities out of obedience, these accomplishments are not from God.

God does not want leaders in the workplace who resort to human power and manipulation. Instead, he wants leaders who follow the example of His Son Jesus, who did not lead through His natural strength, but rather by depending on the Father. He came as a lowly servant. He didn't receive through His natural abilities; He received from obedience to the Father. He was a vessel through whom the Father channeled resources and mighty acts.

These are the kind of men and women that God is raising up today in the workplace. They are not high-profile personalities, but faceless, nameless and humble individuals who seek to follow Jesus completely. They have learned the proper balance between the natural and the spiritual. With this kind of leader, God can transform a workplace or city.

Inquiring of the Lord

In Joshua 9, we read how Joshua and the people of Israel were in the Promised Land, receiving their inheritance from God. No longer in the wasteland of the desert, they were at last enjoying the land of milk and honey that God had promised them. They were winning battles and feeling good about their progress.

God had instructed the Israelites to wipe out all of the inhabitants of the land, for their protection. Everything was going well until one day a band of Gibeonites—one of the groups of people that God had commanded the Israelites to destroy—came by dressed as travelers. They had put worn and patched sandals on their feet and stocked their bags with dry and moldy bread, and they successfully convinced Joshua and his men that they were from a distant country. "The men of Israel sampled their provisions *but did not inquire of the Lord.* Then Joshua made a treaty of peace with them to let them live, and the leaders of the assembly ratified it by oath" (Josh. 9:14-15, emphasis added). Because Joshua did not inquire of the Lord about the Gibeonites, Israel was forced to uphold the peace treaty with their enemy, even though it had been made under false pretenses.

We must be careful as we begin to receive our inheritance from God. We can become lazy when we prosper and begin to operate independently of God. We must keep in mind that God has created us to have a relationship with Him and that He wants us to come to Him for guidance—not because He wants to control us, but because He loves us.

The Promised Land is representative of achievement through obedience versus sweat and toil. Joshua 24:13 describes this: "So I gave you a land on which you did not toil and cities you did not build; and you live in them and eat from vineyards and olive groves that you did not plant." If you are a parent, you know how wonderful it is when your children come to you for advice and they really want it. God is no different. Beware of acting independently in your promised land. God will always want to be involved in your life, and if you rely on Him, He will keep you on track.

How About You?

1. Can you summarize from your own experience the key principle of what it means to receive from God out of obedience versus sweat and toil?

2. What adjustments might be needed for you to begin to walk out this principle?

CHAPTER 11

DO NOT REACH FOR THE POWER

For it is we who are the circumcision, we who worship by the Spirit of God,
who glory in Christ Jesus, and who put no confidence in the flesh.

PHILIPPIANS 3:3

A few years ago, I was asked by a large organization to meet with them about doing some cooperative projects in the Faith at Work area. I visited their headquarters and had some initial discussions. We concluded that we would proceed on a joint conference.

During my visit, I stayed overnight at the headquarters of this ministry, where I was awakened at 5 A.M. and led by the Lord to read Exodus 33:15, which describes Moses' complaint to God about the rebellious Israelites, who had just worshiped the golden calf. Moses said he could not go any further if God did not promise that His presence would go with him. I sensed this was to be our theme for the conference.

Later that morning, I shared that I had received this leading from the Lord regarding the theme of the conference with some of the people in the organization. However, when I shared this with the leader of the organization, he did not take it seriously. I was a bit irritated and my pride was hurt, but I decided to follow a principle that I had been walking in for a few years: *act like you have the authority, but do not reach for the power*. I realized that if God had truly spoken His words into my heart, I would not have to exercise my authority to make it happen. God would orchestrate it.

More discussion was given to the theme, but nothing was resolved. A few hours later, the conference theme came up again. I turned to a friend and read Exodus 33:15 aloud, and he got excited about using that verse as the possible theme of the event. The leader, to my amazement, chimed in as well and said, "Yes, that should be the theme of the conference." It was a big lesson for me.

A few weeks later, I was picking up an intercessor friend from the airport. The moment he got into my car, he said, "The Lord has been speaking to me about the theme of the conference. He gave me Exodus 33:15: 'Then Moses said to him, "If your Presence does not go with us, do not send us up from here."'"

A Paradox

The man or woman who does not perform well on the job is left behind in today's competitive world. Not only is this typical of the world at large, but even many Christians promote the importance of identifying our strengths and encourage us to move in them to accomplish God's will. Yet, throughout the Bible, we are *discouraged* from depending upon our own strengths. Instead, we are urged to rely totally upon the Lord.

This is a paradox. In Philippians 3:3, Paul tells us that we should not put our confidence in the flesh. Psalm 33:16-17 tells us not to put our confidence in things the world considers to be our protection, defense or strength. "No king is saved by the size of his army; no warrior escapes by his great strength. A horse is a vain hope for deliverance; despite all its great strength it cannot save."

So, if we're not supposed to look to the world or to ourselves, who or what are we supposed to depend on? Psalm 33:18-19 continues, "But the eyes of the Lord are on those who fear him, on those whose hope is in his unfailing love, to deliver them from death and keep them alive in famine." This is echoed in Ephesians 6:10, where Paul states, "Finally, be strong in the Lord and in his mighty power."

God wants us to depend upon Him, and He demonstrates this throughout Scripture. For example, in Judges 7, God wouldn't let Gideon fight against another army until he reduced his own from 22,000 soldiers to a mere 300, so that Gideon could not boast about his army's strength. In Joshua 6, God told Joshua to walk around Jericho seven times and blow trumpets instead of relying upon his mighty army to overpower his enemy. In 2 Samuel 24, God judged David when he counted his troops to determine the size of his army's strength, apparently because David took the census out of pride or overconfidence in the strength of his army.

On the other hand, Jesus instructed the disciples in due diligence through the parable of the builder, who is cautioned to consider the cost before beginning to build. "Suppose one of you wants to build a tower. Will he not first sit down and estimate the cost to see if he has enough money to complete it? For if he lays the foundation and is not able to finish it, everyone who sees it will ridicule him, saying, 'This fellow began to build and was not able to finish'" (Luke 14:28-30).

So how do we balance these seeming contradictions?

Withholding Your Natural Gifting

One day I asked my friend and mentor Gunnar Olson, "How in the world do you balance dependence and trust in the Lord while using your God-given talents for His glory?"

"Well, you have asked a very difficult question," he replied. "I have learned one way of checking myself in this area. *I almost have to withhold my natural gifting in certain areas to insure that God is in it.*" His comment was one of those lightning bolts of truth for me.

In the work world, we are trained to press through, no matter the cost. However, perseverance that is not directed by the Holy Spirit is only sweat and toil. We must learn to walk the fine line between these two concepts. On this subject of relying on our human strength, Watchman Nee wrote:

> I believe many people are so rich and strong that they give no ground for God to work. I frequently recall the words, "helpless and hopeless." I must tell God, "all that I have is yours, I myself have nothing. Apart from you I am truly helpless and hopeless." We need to have such a dependent attitude toward God that it is as if we cannot inhale or exhale without Him. In this way we shall see that our power as well as our holiness all come from Him. Oh how God delights in seeing us coming hopeless and helpless to Him. A brother once asked me, "What is the condition for the working of the Spirit?" To which I replied that . . . the Holy Spirit must first bring us to a place where we can do nothing by ourselves. [1]

Of course, God gives us our natural skills and He will use them, although it can be hard at times to tell whether it is God working through us or if it is our natural skill alone making things happen. We need to try to distinguish the difference even as we resist over-analyzing (which can result in paralysis by analysis).

However, the principle is clear in Scripture. The apostle Paul understood that it was not his ability to deliver eloquent sermons that changed people. It was the power of God working through him. In 1 Corinthians 2:3-5, he states, "I came to you in weakness and fear, and with much trembling. My message and my preaching were not with wise and persuasive words, but with a demonstration of the Spirit's power, so that your faith might not rest on men's wisdom, but on God's power." If God's power comes through our work, that brings glory to the Father.

Oswald Chambers understood how God's strength can be expressed through human skills:

> If we do not resolutely cast out the natural, the supernatural can never become natural in us. There are some Christians in whom the supernatural and the natural seem one and the same, and

you say, "Well, they are not one with me. I find the natural at log-gerheads with the spiritual." This is because you have not gone through the fanatical stage of cutting off the right arm, gone through the discipline of maiming the natural, completely casting it out. It is not a question of praying, but performing. For those who have, God has brought the natural back into its right relationship, with the spiritual on top; the spiritual manifests itself in a life which knows no division into sacred and secular.[2]

This principle became real to me when I was seeking to publish my first *TGIF* devotional book. I knew many publishers from working with them through my advertising agency, and I figured getting published would be a simple matter of picking up the phone. So that's what I did. I called a few publishers and immediately got some interest in my book idea. One even gave me a letter of intent to publish, but after a year it finally got dropped, and I was no closer to publishing the book.

I was frustrated. I called other publishers only to become more frustrated. I lamented to Angie almost every day about it. According to her, I talked about publishing the book to everything that breathed—which is a bit of an exaggeration, but not far from the truth. I even considered self-publishing until she threatened my life (we were still very much in a financial crisis). One day, as she was walking out the door to go to work, I brought up my frustration again. She had finally had it. She turned and asked, "Os, have you finished *writing* the book?"

"No, I have about 60 more devotionals to write" I replied.

With a hint of irritation in her voice, she said, "When you finish writing the book, God will give you a publisher." Her words were not what I wanted to hear, but the firmness with which she shut the door made me stop and think. I took her advice and stopped pursuing publishers, and then simply began working on finishing the book.

A short while after, I began doing business with a few publishers on another matter. Eventually, an acquisitions editor proposed that we meet in a few months. On the day of the meeting, the publishing company offered me a two-book contract. Amazingly, that was the day I wrote the 365th devotional! On my way home, I remembered the words

Angie had spoken to me a few months earlier. Now I had to admit that Angie was the prophet in the family!

What I learned from this experience was that God did indeed want to have my work published, but that He wanted to guide me in the process in such a way that He would receive glory from the process itself.

Laying Down Natural Gifts to Witness God's Power

Crystal Alman is a businesswoman who manufactures designer clothing in Colombia, South America. Her designs are known for their elaborate detail and the accessories sewn onto the clothing. A major retail chain agreed to carry her clothing line based on the merits of its unique and original styling and requested four designs to consider for the next season. She was given a particular deadline, which was going to be very difficult to meet.

When the deadline came, Crystal had not had the time to finish the elaborate final detailing work on two of the pieces. She called the retailer and said she had two pieces ready to ship, but that she needed more time to complete the other two pieces. The retailer argued with her, however, and said, "Send them to us anyway."

Now, Crystal is a perfectionist. It made her uncomfortable to send something to the retailer that did not display her high level of creativity and quality. Then she recalled the idea of withholding our natural ability in order to depend on God's power. So, in total opposition to her natural inclination, she sent the two "unfinished" pieces of clothing to the retailer along with the other two "finished" pieces.

After a little time had passed, Crystal received a phone call from the retailer. To her amazement, he chose the two pieces of clothing that she had considered to be unfinished and declined the other two.

This was a great lesson for Crystal. She knew that God was demonstrating His power through this principle of withholding her natural gifting to show her it was by His hand that she was being successful in her business. This did not take away her need to be creative or skillful, but enabled her to come to a new understanding of the need to place greater dependence upon obedience to God than on her own natural reasoning.

Paul Cuny has a similar story. Paul was a builder in Jacksonville, Florida. In 1980, he believed that he was being led by God to work with a large ministry to help direct several significant construction projects for them. This became a time of severe testing for Paul, and even though he wanted to leave hundreds of times, the Lord would not release him.

As the projects for the ministry began to wind down, Paul was asked to stay on for future projects. To keep him busy, he was given a number of jobs, one of which was cleaning toilets. Morning after morning, he would go into the men's room, lock the door, get down on his knees and complain to the Lord, "I'm a college graduate! How can You have me cleaning these toilets? Remember me?"

Though Paul knew that the Lord had called him to work with this ministry, he realized one morning that he could not go on like this. He finally told the Lord, "I will not leave here until You promote me. I ask only one thing—that You give me contentment with my circumstance, or I cannot go on another day." Each morning, he would ask the Lord to give him this contentment with his circumstance, and each morning, heavenly manna would come down to him. The manna only lasted 24 hours, at which time Paul would have to go back to the Lord and ask for it again.

In spite of this new contentment from the Lord, Paul still felt totally forgotten by God and that he could be of no use to Him. This went on for almost a year, until one morning the Lord spoke to him during his quiet time and said, "You have been promoted!" Paul turned in his resignation that morning.

A few months later, Paul received a phone call from a man in the Midwest who owned five successful businesses. He wanted to interview Paul for a position that involved running a construction and development company for his investment group. The call came as a total surprise to Paul. As he drove to the interview, he told the Lord, "I only want your will in my life, nothing else. I am content to remain obscure for the rest of my life if I have You. I am not going to promote myself to this man. I will give this man no reason to hire me. You must override my lack of experience for me to get this job.'"

As the meeting got underway, the businessman, without looking up from his notepad, asked Paul the first question of the interview: "If I asked you to clean a toilet, what would you do?"

Paul sat there, stunned. He recalls, "Inside, I was trying to control myself, as I wanted to burst out laughing." Paul assured him that he would simply pick up a sponge and start cleaning.

To everyone's amazement, Paul was hired. From his perspective, he was a nobody and the least likely to be given this coveted and cherished position. "I didn't deserve it or earn it," Paul states. "I was not qualified for it and if I tried, I could not possibly have orchestrated those events. In spite of all this, the hand of God was on me and everything I did was mightily blessed."

The projects were an astounding success. After several months of what Paul considered his dream job, he asked his boss why he hired him instead of all the others. His boss replied, "Paul, I still have a large stack of applications from people who wanted this job. Do you remember the first question I asked you in the interview? I asked every one of them the same question and you were the only one who said he would clean the toilet. Paul, I am a wealthy man, but I grew up dirt poor. I clean my own toilets at home. I can't have people running my businesses who are too proud to clean a toilet."

This is an amazing story of God's faithfulness to a man who was willing to lay down his own natural ability in order to receive God's power in his life. It took a year of cleaning toilets to get to that point, but when Paul finally got to the place where nothing mattered to him except pleasing God, he was promoted.

God wants to show us that He is involved in all aspects of our lives. But He also wants us to know that it is by His hand. This requires relinquishing control at times and stepping back and waiting for his timing. If you are going to be a leader in the kingdom of God like Gideon or Joshua or David, you must learn how to withhold your natural gifting at times to insure that God is your source. God will receive greater glory and the fruit will last longer.

The Temptation of Pride

When we begin to accumulate wealth, manage other people or become known for our workplace expertise, we are most susceptible to falling to the most devious sin in God's eyes—pride. Pride is the greatest temptation to a successful workplace minister. As soon as we move into the place where we begin to think more highly of ourselves than we should, God says he will take action—sometimes strong action!

> You may say to yourself, "My power and the strength of my hands have produced this wealth for me" . . . If you ever forget the Lord your God and follow other gods and worship and bow down to them, I testify against you today that you will surely be destroyed. Like the nations the Lord destroyed before you, so you will be destroyed for not obeying the Lord your God (Deut. 8:17,19-20).

God's strong words to the Israelites demonstrate His utter impatience toward those who are too proud of what they have accomplished. God gives us the skill, the intelligence, the resources, the energy, the drive and the opportunities to accomplish something. Yet when we become prideful, He will begin a process of reproof in our lives. In King David, we see a man who had a mature understanding of God's activity in his life. He was totally sold out to the purposes of God for his life and his resources. He wanted to honor God by building a temple for Him. However, God said he would not build it; instead, he told David, "Your son, whom I will put on the throne in your place will build the temple for my Name" (1 Kings 5:5).

At the end of David's life, he makes a profound statement as he is about to give millions of dollars worth of gold and other precious items for the new temple: "But who am I, and who are my people, that we should be able to give as generously as this? Everything comes from you, and *we have given you only what comes from your hand*" (1 Chron. 29:14-15, emphasis added). David had learned this important principle of receiving only what God gave him. He gave out of a humble heart that knew the source of his wealth and power.

Examine your heart today to see whether you have fallen victim to pride. Are you sharing what God has entrusted to you with God's people or to the needy? Are you being an instrument of God's blessing to others? What areas of pride may have crept into your life? Ask the Lord to show you today.

Avoid being put on the shelf or cast aside because of your own pride. Make a decision to commit your way to the Lord and ask Him to guide you in achieving your goals. To be successful in your life—including your 9 to 5 life—you need to stop relying on your own efforts and ask God to keep you humbly reliant upon Him.

How About You?

1. Can you describe the difference between using your natural skill and waiting for God's timing to orchestrate an outcome? How have you seen this in your own life?

2. What is the greatest challenge for you to live out this principle?

CHAPTER 12

MIRACLES AT WORK

The apostles performed many miraculous signs and wonders among the people.

ACTS 5:12

In chapter 1, we noted that God wanted to use Moses' staff to perform miracles. When God told Moses, *"Take this staff* in your hand so you can perform miraculous signs with it" (Exod. 4:17, emphasis added), He was really telling Moses that He was going to use Moses' vocation and perform miracles through it. I want to remind you that God also wants to use your staff—your vocation—to perform miracles. This is not only so that you will know the power of God, but also so that others around you will know it as well.

As I travel around the world, I see a new breed of believer—those who experience the power of Christ in their workplace callings. These individuals are experiencing miracles that manifest the kingdom of God in their workplaces. As you read each of the following true stories, remember that God also wants to use your work to perform miracles, so that it too will bring glory to Him and others will come to understand His power.

The Miracle of Faith

Several years ago, God performed a miracle for Gunnar Olson in his business. Gunnar owns a plastics company in Sweden, called Alfapac, which makes huge plastic bags that are used to cover bales of hay in the farmlands across Europe.

It was the harvest season, and Alfapac was getting ready to ship thousands of pallets of these bags to its customers. Then an alarming discovery was made. Gunnar arrived at his office and was greeted by his younger brother, who was in charge of running the daily operations. "Well, I guess we have come to the end of Alfapac," he said.

"What in the world are you talking about?" asked Gunnar.

"Every bag on the warehouse floor has been sealed shut from top to bottom," his brother lamented. "We have already had scientists come to inspect them. They say some type of molecular breakdown has occurred that allowed the bags to seal into a solid sheet of plastic. They say our entire stock is trash. Nothing can be done." They both knew that this would mean the end of their company.

Gunnar went home and shared this catastrophe with his family, and they sought the Lord in prayer. After they prayed, they took turns speaking up about the things they felt that the Lord had put on their hearts. His wife said, "If God can turn water into wine, what are plastics?" His daughter said, "I don't believe this is from the Lord. We should stand against it."

But it has already happened, Gunnar thought to himself. At that moment, a Scripture came into his mind: "If you have faith as small as a mustard seed, you can say to this mountain, 'Move from here to there' and it will move. Nothing will be impossible for you" (Matt. 17:20). So, Gunnar felt the Lord was leading them to take a stand against the enemy and to expect some sort of miracle. After his family sensed this leading, the burden of the situation was released from them and they decided to go to the factory on Sunday to pray.

In the meantime, Gunnar called his brother and told him to take the weekend off to play golf. His brother's response was understandable: "How can you say that when you're ruined?"

"Well, there's no problem anymore," Gunnar replied. He had complete peace that the Lord would come through.

On Sunday afternoon, Gunnar went to the factory with his family. He stood outside the factory and in a very loud voice declared, "Listen heaven! Listen Earth! Who is the Lord over Alfapac? His name is Jesus! In the name of Jesus, we command that the molecules migrate back!" He and the family then proceeded to lay hands on each of the pallets to pray for restoration of the plastic bags. It took them three hours.

The next morning, when the employees began to inspect the bags, they discovered that every single bag had been restored to its original condition! Scientists were called in to validate this incredible miracle at the plastic bag factory, and the story spread all over Europe to the glory of God.

The Miracle of God's Love

I show a video clip of Gunnar's plastic bag story as part of my one-day Called to the Workplace workshop. Gunnar's testimony was moving and memorable to Donny Godsey, a small business owner who was in the audience one day. Later, when he had his own crisis in his business, he remembered Gunnar's testimony and decided to exercise a similar kind of faith. He wrote me the following letter about the miracle in his workplace that God gave to him:

> I own a video company that shoots a variety of projects. One day, my editor discovered a videographer's worst nightmare—a garbled mess of video picture and little or no audio on tapes that I had shot the weekend before. Four tapes of raw footage from two separate events were ruined. There was no recourse except to explain to the clients what happened, offer them their money back and find another line of work.
>
> Then I remembered how Gunnar Olson prayed over an impossible situation and God delivered him. My situation was very similar. So I got my editor and my family together and we prayed that God would alter the digital tapes. I got an odd sense

of peace and knew God had answered my prayer. I relayed to the group that I believed God had told me that the tapes would be fine in a day.

"You have got to be kidding me," my editor laughed. "God doesn't need time to fix something. Put a tape in!" So I put a tape in the editing deck, and right before our eyes, the tape now had a perfectly clear picture and audio where there had been no sound moments before. I let out a joyful shout that drew my wife back into the room to see the miracle as well.

Excitedly, I popped another tape, but it was still damaged. I decided to check the others the next day. Later that night, God seemed to be drawing me to the tapes once again, so I played one. Sure enough, it was fixed as well. I went absolutely crazy with excitement. The other two tapes, however, remained damaged.

The next morning, I entered my editing room with great anticipation. I put in one of the remaining damaged tapes that contained footage from a wedding, but the video was still scrambled and there was no audio. My wife heard me and came in to look over my shoulder. I prayed out loud over the ruined footage and reassured my wife that God loves us and would take care of things. She reminded me that He fixed two out of four tapes, and that may be all He does. Yet I remembered that God said the tapes would be fixed in a day, so I kept praying as I watched the screen.

The bride was now coming down the aisle and the footage was still useless. Then suddenly, before our eyes, the tape began to clear up. Everything got set right, just as the pastor announced how good God is and how much He intimately loves us. I forwarded through the tape to see if the signal remained clear. It did. I turned to look at my wife, who had tears streaming down her face. Apparently, God had rigged this moment to touch her deeply on issues that only the two of them knew about. Not only did God save my business, but He also ministered to my family through this crisis-fixing miracle.

The Miracle of Invention

George Washington Carver was born into slavery and grew up at the height of racial discrimination at the close of the Civil War. Yet he overcame all these obstacles to become one of the most influential men in the history of the United States. Persevering through many trials, Carver ended up with several agricultural degrees.

The economy of the farming south had been devastated by years of civil war and the fact that the plantations no longer employed slave labor. Decades of growing only cotton and tobacco had depleted the soils of the southern United States. Carver was able to convince the southern farmers to plant peanuts and sweet potatoes, instead of cotton, to replenish the soil. This led to his greatest trial. When the farmers began to grow peanuts and sweet potatoes, they lost even more money because there was no market for these crops.

Carver cried out daily to the Lord, "Why did you make the peanut!" and each day God would give him new ideas on ways to use the peanut. He ultimately discovered some 300 marketable products from the peanut and hundreds of uses for soybeans, pecans and sweet potatoes, and his contributions were a key part to helping the region recover.

Carver did not patent or profit from most of his products, but freely gave his discoveries to mankind. "God gave them to me," he would say about his ideas. "How can I sell them to someone else?" He was offered six-figure income opportunities from Henry Ford and became friends with presidents of his day, yet he never became wealthy. His epitaph read, "He could have added fortune to fame, but caring for neither, he found happiness and honor in being helpful to the world."[1]

Miraculous Protection

Boet Pretorius is a farmer in Zimbabwe, Africa, where there had been much turmoil. Many farmers had lost their lives and their farms due to militant political initiatives in the country. Boet was faced with the same prospect.

At one point, Boet was visited by the head of police and war veterans who accused him of training militia on his farm. However, they found that the only training that was going on was spiritual, for Boet taught the Bible to his workers on his farm. Nevertheless, death threats were made against him and he was informed that he was on a hit list of a militant government group. Boet and his family lived in constant fear, and they often spent nights at his neighbors' houses.

Boet began to pray about this fear. The Lord spoke to him and said, "You fear because you declare that you have died and live in Me, yet you live apart from Me. The threats are not against you as a person but against Christ in you; against the body of Christ." Boet repented about allowing the fear to grip him and returned to the farm and remained there. The war vets returned and demanded $500,000 in Zimbabwe dollars to take him off their hit list. Boet prayed with his workers on the farm, and the Lord replied, "If you walk in the light, you walk in God's protection." He refused to pay the money, and as a result the war vets kidnapped him and threatened his life.

During this time, God was speaking to Boet about dying to himself and giving up all his rights. As soon as Boet felt submission to the will of God in his heart, the Lord opened an opportunity for him to share the gospel with his captors. The leader wept and asked Boet for a Bible. The war vets released him, but his troubles were not over.

A few days later, about 70 other people invaded the farm during a heavy rainstorm. The farmers were always advised not to let these people in behind their security fences, as they might never be able to get them out. Yet when Boet and his workers prayed, they felt that they should offer these people shelter and food, so he opened the barns to the invaders.

The next night, Boet showed these invaders the Campus Crusade for Christ film called *Jesus*, and many accepted Christ. The following morning, Boet discovered that his workers had been praying and counseling the invaders all night long and had not slept all night. A few days later, the invaders came to Boet, announced they were going home and invited him to visit their people to share the gospel with them. The invaders proclaimed that his farm belonged to Jesus, and they left without harming

Boet or any of his workers. God had performed miracles after Boet submitted to Him. It was a great testimony to his workers and the invaders who came to harm him.

The Miracle of Healing

Larry and Rose Ihle own a dental lab in Minneapolis, Minnesota. In addition to using the business as a means of serving the Lord, Larry and Rose also serve in a prayer ministry in their conservative denominational church. One Sunday, Rose came into the prayer room to report that there was a man in the foyer who needed prayer. Larry went upstairs to look for the man and discovered he was in a wheelchair. Larry greeted him warmly and asked, "May we pray for you?"

The man opened his mouth, but was only able to mutter in a very bad stutter, "y . . . ye . . . yes. I wo . . . wou . . . would like that." Larry helped the man to the prayer room.

As Larry looked at the man, he had an overwhelming sense that he was to pray a prayer of deliverance from a "spirit of stutter." Meanwhile, some ladies of the church were looking on, wondering what he was doing. Prayers of deliverance were not normally a part of this conservative church. Larry began to pray, "In the name of Jesus, spirit of stutter, come out of him!" Larry immediately felt the pressure of the situation. *What if nothing happens?* he thought.

After Larry finished saying this prayer, the man still stuttered as before. So Larry prayed again, "In the name of Jesus, spirit of stutter, come out of him!" He waited a few moments and then asked the man a question. The man answered—with no stutter. As Larry talked to the man, they both realized that something miraculous had happened. The man no longer stuttered. God had healed him, but Larry still felt there was more to pray for.

"How long have you been in a wheelchair?" Larry asked.

"Since I was 12 years old," replied the man (he was now 53 years old).

Larry asked if he wanted to walk. The man said he did. Larry looked into his eyes and said a simple prayer: "In the name of Jesus, stand up."

The man made an effort to stand up from his wheelchair. His arms began to shake as he moved upward. He stood up, shaky and unsure, but standing. He could not believe what he was doing. He was standing by himself for the first time since he was 12 years old!

The man began to take baby steps around the room. He was walking. He was walking! God had done a great miracle in this man who thought he was simply coming to another church service to hear a sermon. God had changed his life through a businessman who was willing to pray for the miraculous.

Larry asked the man to stay for the service and invited him to sit in the front pew. The man responded, "If you don't mind, I believe I will just stand."

Larry is a good friend of mine, and recently he took me to his church to meet with the church staff. He introduced me to a man standing at the information booth, whom he referred to as the "miracle man." I was delighted to meet the man who had been in the wheelchair, but who now walks and talks without a stutter.

The Miracle of Evangelism

A cab driver in the Philippines got radically saved. He was taught that he now had the power of God in his life to transform his community. Because he had not had any prior religious training to the contrary, he took a literal approach to believing what the Bible says about prayer and miracles.

He decided that the best mission field for him was the local bar in his neighborhood. So he began to visit this bar to find the most qualified sinner he could find in order to minister to him. He met the bartender and determined that he was a great prospect because he was also a gay drug addict and a pimp to 35 prostitutes. The cab driver visited the bar regularly and got to know the bartender while drinking his "usual"—a Coke. Eventually, the Lord used the cab driver to win this man to Christ.

The power of God moved greatly in the bartender, and he was delivered from his homosexual lifestyle. He began to change his life and share

Jesus with the prostitutes. All 35 of them became Christians, and they began meeting in the bar for Bible study.

Soon, the owner of the bar began to notice the change in these people, and he also was saved. The bar became a church, and the group started 10 cell group churches in the neighborhood. That is a miraculous transformation![2]

No matter what situation we find ourselves in, we should always remain aware that God might want to intervene. He desires a moment-by-moment relationship with us, and sometimes He wants to demonstrate His loving power. We can approach God about any situation, for there is nothing that is too small or too great for Him.

Miracles at *your* workplace? Yes!

How About You?

1. Have you ever experienced a miracle as you have used your vocation? How did it happen?
2. Why do you think we don't experience more miracles in our workplaces?

TRANSFORMING A CITY

I have given them the glory that you gave me, that they may be one
as we are one: I in them and you in me.

J O H N   1 7 : 2 2 - 2 3

Can a city be truly transformed for Jesus Christ? Does it seem like such a lofty goal that few will ever attain it? Well the reality is that today there are no fewer than 200 cities across the world that are in some form of transformation, according to Alistair Petrie, who spoke at the 2004 International Coalition of Workplace Ministries (ICWM) Workplace Transformation Summit. Petrie cited these cities as having a level of transformation in every aspect of their public, governmental and business life.

Webster's Dictionary defines transformation this way: "to change in nature, disposition, heart, or the like; to convert . . . a thorough or radical change."[1] A transformed city is the answer to Jesus' prayer: "Your kingdom come, your will be done on earth as it is in heaven" (Matt. 6:10). It is God's kingdom manifested here on Earth. What does a transformed city look like? It is one that has experienced a spiritual awakening or revival, a declining crime rate and an increase in economic stability.

Workplace Leaders Are Key to City Transformation

One of the first cities in the Bible to be transformed was Sychar, in Samaria, when the Samaritan woman met Jesus at the town well. As we read in John 4:7-26, when Jesus revealed to the woman that He knew she had had five husbands, she was amazed and came to believe in Him. She shared her newfound faith with others in the city, and "many of the Samaritans from that town believed in him because of the woman's testimony" (John 4:39).

One of the first things that must take place for a city to be transformed is that Jesus must be invited into that city through the city "gatekeepers." This is what happened in Sychar and what is happening in cities where transformation is taking place today. One such city is Kampala, in Uganda. At one point, 33.3 percent of the population of Uganda had AIDS. The World Health Organization predicted that the nation's economy would collapse by the year 2000 because there would be only widows and orphans left. So people sought the Lord and prayed. The results?

New city leaders invited Jesus into their city to be Lord over it. Christians have replaced the evil dictatorship of Idi Amin, whose brutality in the 1970s led to the executions of hundreds of thousands of people and plunged the nation into chaos and poverty. Today, the people in Parliament pray, the police fax prayer requests to judges, and a major bank even plays praise music on all 11 floors. In some communities, crime is down 70 percent and AIDS has dropped to 5 percent.[2]

Another important step is that the city must repent of its sins. Jesus went into the cities and did great miracles. Yet many of those cities did not repent, and this angered the Lord. "Then Jesus began to denounce the cities in which most of his miracles had been performed, because they did not repent" (Matt. 11:20).

Workplace leaders are important to city transformation because they are often in places of power to make changes. Dr. Peter Wagner makes the following observations in the foreword to my book, *The Faith@Work Movement*:

For years we have sought after transformation of our cities. We have prayed, held pastor prayer conferences, prayer-walked our cities, etc. Still, not one U.S. city has been transformed. Why is that? I feel I finally know the answer to that question. It lies in the fact that pastors and church leaders do not hold the authority in the cities where the change must originate. Business and government leaders hold that authority. So, until we in the church equip and release the apostles in the workplace, we will never see our cities transformed by Jesus Christ.[3]

Dawie Spangenberg and his wife, Isebel, lead a worldwide prayer initiative called Transformation Africa. He once made a startling comment to a Christian workplace lunch group in Atlanta: "If a business owner is operating a business in a city and is not directly involved in transforming that city, he is raping that city. He needs to leave that city!" These are strong words, but Spangenberg is convinced that business leaders need to stop trying to see what a business can do for them, start determining why God gave them their business, and then seek to build the kingdom of God in their communities.

The problem that exists today is that workplace apostles are not being recognized—nor do they even recognize themselves. They have not seen their careers as holy callings and have not understood the redemptive nature of their work and calling. Consequently, they often resign themselves to being financiers of God's work instead of being major catalysts for transformation of their workplaces and cities. And yet, when a man or a woman becomes willing to be used in the context of the workplace, God can accomplish a great deal.

Jeremiah Lanphier is a good example of what I'm talking about. He was a businessman in New York City in the mid-1800s. A simple prayer, a willing heart and an act of obedience resulted in city transformation throughout the United States. Here's his story:

In a small, darkened room, in the back of one of New York City's lesser churches, a man prayed alone. His request of God was simple, but earth-shattering: "Lord, what wilt Thou have me to do?"

He was a man approaching midlife, without a wife or family, but he had financial means. He had made a decision to reject the "success syndrome" that drove the city's businessmen and bankers. God used this businessman to turn New York City's commercial empire on its head. He began a businessmen's prayer meeting on September 23, 1857.

The meetings began slowly, but within a few months 20 noonday meetings were convening daily throughout the city. The *New York Tribune* and the *New York Herald* issued articles of revival. It had become the city's biggest news. Now a full-fledged revival, it moved outside New York. By spring of 1858, 2,000 met daily in Chicago's Metropolitan Theatre, and in Philadelphia the meetings mushroomed into a four-month long tent meeting. Meetings were held in Baltimore, Washington, Cincinnati, Chicago, New Orleans, and Mobile. Thousands met to pray because one man stepped out. This was an extraordinary move of God through one man.[4]

Learning from a Pioneer

When it comes to city transformation, it is hard to write about the subject without acknowledging Ed Silvoso, founder and president of Harvest Evangelism. He is one of the modern-day pioneers and a leading authority on the subject. His books *My City, God's City; Prayer Evangelism;* and *Anointed for Business* are three must-read titles. Ed became more involved directly with the workplace movement in 2002, when he saw how important the workplace was to reaching a city. He has discovered four ingredients that must be in place for us to begin to change the spiritual climate in a city. These include:

1. *Speaking peace to the lost.* Blessing opens the door to unbiased fellowship.
2. *Fellowshipping with them.* Fellowship establishes a level of trust, allowing our neighbors to share with us their felt needs.

3. *Taking care of their needs.* Prayer addresses these felt needs.
4. *Proclaim the good news.* When we intercede for our neighbors, God comes near them in a tangible way.[5]

Ed Silvoso's ministry has a proven track record that originates from his work in Resistencia, Argentina. In 1990, this city of 400,000 had an estimated 5,100 believers scattered among 70 congregations (68 of which were the result of a church split). The city was notorious for being a spiritual cemetery. However, today there are over 100,000 Christians in the city and 220,000 in the province, making it the most evangelical province in the nation.

Silvoso reports breakthroughs in Argentina at high levels of government and business. In the fall of 2004, he made his annual trip to Argentina with a group of marketplace leaders and intercessors. During that trip, the president of a political party received the Lord and invited Jesus to be the head of it; the entire management team of the Argentine equivalent of the Mayo Clinic received the Lord and invited Jesus into the clinic; and the Argentine equivalent of Donald Trump and his wife—one of the most influential couples in the nation—received the Lord and invited Jesus to be the CEO of their business group.[6]

Silvoso cites the workplace (which he terms the "marketplace") as key to winning a city for Jesus Christ:

The heart of the city is not the Church, much less than the church building. The Church is the light of the city, but the heart is in the marketplace. Cities are often known by a signature skyline made up of buildings that represent the leading corporations in town. This is where the actions needs to be if we are to reach our cities.

The first European convert was a businesswoman who dealt in expensive apparel (see Acts 16:14,15). This was immediately followed by a power encounter in the marketplace involving a slave girl with a spirit of divination (see Acts 16:16-21). Luke recounts 22 power encounters in the book of Acts—all of them but one happened in nonreligious meetings, most of them in the marketplace. These events had a profound effect on the cities and, in some cases, the outlying regions.

For a city to be transformed, the marketplace must be transformed. The marketplace is where the battle for our cities should be fought, and there is an army already in place that needs to be commissioned and empowered: the so-called laity. Whether they run corporations or work for them, they are better positioned (than the clergy) to transform the marketplace.

Christians in the marketplace already have an anointing to share the gospel with the lost; but, in most cases, the anointing has not been activated, as the laypersons have been relegated to the second-class status in the church.[7]

What is Required for City Transformation?

There are four key ingredients required to see a city transformed. These include prayer, humility, unity and knowledge of God's ways. Let's discuss each of these in turn.

Prayer
In every city in which transformation has taken place, believers have come together to pray for their city. Prayer changes the spiritual climate of a city. Some of the main areas of influence that must be the focus of our prayers include churches and businesses; the legal, political, educational and medical fields; and the media/entertainment industry. "If my people, who are called by my name, will humble themselves and pray and seek my face and turn from their wicked ways, then will I hear from heaven and will forgive their sin and will heal their land" (2 Chron. 7:14). Workplace leaders must he strategically aligned with intercessors to impact their city.

Humility
God uses men and women who recognize that they need each other and who do not seek glory for their work. "He guides the humble in what is

right and teaches them his way" (Ps. 25:9). The workplace leaders that God is using today care little about being in the limelight. They have a Kingdom perspective that avoids bringing attention to themselves or any one group in order to impact the city for Jesus Christ.

Unity

Jesus said, "May they be brought to complete unity to let the world know that you sent me and have loved them even as you have loved me" (John 17:23). God calls each of us individually and corporately to represent Christ to the world, but our independence, pride and egos often prevent us from becoming unified in the purposes of Christ. We are scattered in our church affiliations and in our city transformation efforts. Unity is built when we roll up our sleeves and determine to work together—pastors, priests and people from every walk of life. The marketplace and the Church must come together to bless the city with practical initiatives that benefit the city.

Knowledge of God's Ways

Those of us in the workplace are often zealous for God, but we can move in presumption instead of in a faith that is rooted in knowledge of God's ways. Such was the case of David, who wanted to bring the Ark of the Covenant into the city of Jerusalem. He was zealous for God and celebrated as he brought the Ark into the city. However, the ark was being carried into the city on a cart instead of by priests on poles, as God required. When a man named Uzzah reached out to catch the Ark when the oxen stumbled, he was immediately struck dead by God. "When they came to the threshing floor of Nacon, Uzzah reached out and took hold of the ark of God, because the oxen stumbled. The Lord's anger burned against Uzzah because of his irreverent act; therefore God struck him down and he died there beside the ark of God" (2 Sam 6:6-7). David was devastated.

We must connect with our priests and pastors to jointly work on bringing the presence of God into our cities. Otherwise, we will fail like David and be guilty of presumption. "For I can testify about them that they are zealous for God, but their zeal is not based on knowledge" (Romans 10:2).

City Transformation "Trinity"

I also believe there is a city transformation "trinity," if you will allow me to use that word in this way. I believe three groups of people are vital to bringing change to the spiritual climate in a city: (1) intercessors, who are called to intercede for the city; (2) apostolic nuclear church leaders, who are church leaders with a vision for their cities; and (3) marketplace leaders, or more specifically, workplace apostles. These are men and women called to impact their cities through their spheres of influence in government, business and education.

In 2003, the Lord began to impress upon me that I was to start bringing the workplace leaders and ministries together in the city of Atlanta for a vision of transforming the city. We partnered with the Billy Graham Evangelistic Association in April 2004 to host a workplace conference for the city. However, nothing really sparked any ongoing initiatives from that meeting.

I continued to meet with the workplace ministries, but nothing seemed to be happening. I kept trying to find intercessors in the city, but I was unsuccessful. Finally, I got to know Alistair Petrie when I had him speak at our international conference in October 2004. Alistair is an authority and researcher on city transformation. When I shared my frustration with him, he said, "Oh, you need to meet Jacquie Tyre. She is your city intercessor." I met with Jacquie, and things immediately began to happen. I began connecting with some of the city church leaders.

A short time later, in February 2005, Graham Power, founder of Transformation Africa and the Global Day of Prayer, came through town. I was asked to host a meeting for Graham to share the vision of the Global Day of Prayer. Up to this point, the city had not made any decisions about joining this initiative; but that day about 100 leaders in the city came to hear Graham and by the end of the meeting made a commitment to hold an Atlanta Global Day of Prayer. Things started moving fast. Within 30 days $125,000 was raised, a 20,000-seat venue was reserved and the city began coming together.

I believe the reason that all this happened is because these three groups of people came together in a unified effort to impact our city—

intercessors, apostolic church leaders and workplace leaders.

God Is Birthing City Coalitions

City coalitions are forming in larger cities around the United States, as well as internationally. These coalitions usually include workplace leaders, pastors, non-profit workplace ministries and intercessors. When you combine these four groups of people, you have a very strong core of leadership that can impact a city. However, the challenge is bringing these leaders together in such a way that there is real unity.

Rick Boxx is a workplace leader in Kansas City who saw the need to begin such a coalition. "I felt the Lord leading me to develop a citywide model that would be effective in living out John 17," he says. "The desire to see a unified effort between the different ministries and business leaders who have influence over the workplaces of Kansas City led me to contact several of them for our first meeting. We determined to begin meeting on a regular basis to see what God might do with this group." Their first cooperative dinner meeting had more than 600 in attendance. They are now seeking God's vision for transformation in their city. Similar coalitions are now under way in many cities, including Atlanta, Georgia; Raleigh, North Carolina; Austin, Texas; Spartanburg, South Carolina; San Marco, California; Chicago, Illinois; Minneapolis, Minnesota, and in the San Francisco Bay area in California, just to name a few.

The Bible says that we are called to disciple the nations. You cannot disciple a nation until you disciple a city and the people in that city. I believe that God has begun to move upon His people in the cities, for the sake of the nations.

How About You?

1. Do you think a city can be transformed for Jesus Christ? Why or why not?
2. What would your workplace or city look like if it were to be transformed by Jesus Christ? List three things that would be different.

CHAPTER 14

FROM THE WORKPLACE TO THE NATIONS

Do you see a man skilled in his work? He will serve before kings;
he will not serve before obscure men.

PROVERBS 22:29

The International Christian Chamber of Commerce (ICCC) conference was about to begin. There were about 400 business people from 75 different nations in the room. After a time of worship, a man stood up and exhorted (actually, it was more like a rebuke) Christians in the United States to pray for their president. It was a difficult time in our nation, and Bill Clinton was not the most esteemed person in the opinion of many Americans.

The man who challenged us to pray was pastor Romain Zannou from the small African nation of Benin. Romain had earned the right to exhort us. Many years ago, God had given him a burden to pray for his Marxist dictator president, Mathieu Kerekou. For 10 years, he prayed for two hours a day for Kerekou's salvation and for God to give Kerekou wisdom to lead the nation. One day while he was praying, Romain felt that the Lord had a message for the president. Within 24 hours, he was standing in a room with Kerekou to deliver the word of the Lord.

After the dismantling of the U.S.S.R., Kerekou decided to hold free elections, and he was defeated. Though he and Romain had agreed to meet after the elections for a time of Bible study, the former president refused to meet with Romain after only a few meetings. Almost every day after that, Romain went to Kerekou's home, only to be told that Kerekou did not wish to see him. Each day he said, "I will wait," and stood outside the wall for hours, in hopes that Kerekou would let him in.

After a year and a half of these unsuccessful visits, the former president finally received him and greeted him with the words, "Pastor Zannou, you are a very persistent man." They began an in-depth study of the Bible, sometimes studying for six hours at a time. Through this study of the word of God, the former president received Christ.

In 1997, during the Global Conference on World Evangelism in South Africa, re-elected President Kerekou addressed 600 business people from all over the world who were meeting with one goal in mind—to fulfill the Great Commission through their influence in the workplace. He shared his vision for Benin to become a Christian nation and asked for their help. Several people have since helped develop many initiatives on behalf of the nation of Benin.

Romain Zannou is one of many unknown leaders who have a passion for Jesus and who are being used to impact nations through their own workplace calling. They are an unlikely group of people—pastors, flower shop owners, builders, industrialists and even a former golf pro (me). This chapter profiles various case studies of God's transforming power among the nations and the people He is using to do it. My hope and prayer is that it will encourage you to dream big!

Thinking Big

It was 4:00 A.M. in Cape Town, South Africa, in July 2000 when businessman Graham Power was awakened by a vision from God that came in three distinct parts. In the first part of the vision, God instructed

Graham to rent the 45,000-seat Newlands rugby stadium in Cape Town for a day of repentance and prayer for that city. In the second part of the vision, he saw the prayer movement spreading to the rest of South Africa for a national day of prayer. In the final part of the vision, he saw the prayer effort spread to cover the rest of the continent.

Graham was obedient to the vision, and on March 21, 2001, a capacity crowd gathered in the Newlands rugby stadium for prayer and repentance. Soon after, a notorious gangster in the city was saved. News of the first gathering spread quickly, and in 2002, eight cities in South Africa hosted a day of prayer. Leading up to the event, young people from all over the country took part in a "walk of hope" from Bloemfontein to the eight stadiums where the prayer meetings were to be held. The events were broadcast on television.

Then in May 2004, 20 to 30 million Africans from all 53 countries in Africa and five islands gathered for united prayer in hundreds of stadiums throughout the continent. This was followed by a worldwide day of prayer involving all seven continents. Hundreds of transformation stories throughout the continent of Africa have resulted from this major effort, which all started with the obedience of one businessman.

An Invitation from Israel

In 2002, the ICCC cohosted a business congress with the nation of Israel. Three Israeli departments of trade and commerce came together with 450 other business leaders from over 40 nations for one reason: to bless the nation of Israel at a time when the Israelis most needed it—the eighth year of the *intifada* (the armed uprising of Palestinians against the Israeli occupation of the West Bank and the Gaza Strip). The Israeli leaders were so impressed with the Christians that they invited ICCC to establish their headquarters in Jerusalem. The relationship is continuing to develop in conjunction with a number of other joint projects.

The Egyptian Business Community in Cairo saw the success of this event and asked ICCC to do the same for them. The ICCC brought the

International Community to Cairo in February 2005 for an international business expo and business matchmaking event to promote commerce, export, investment and the small and medium business sector in Egypt. It was an unprecedented event for a Christian-based group to partner with a primarily Muslim nation. You won't hear much of this on the evening news.

China: Transforming the Educational System

"You Can Start a Business" is a video series that ICCC has developed and promoted in China since 1999. As China began moving toward a market-driven economy, the government started looking for someone to help train their young people in that area. IBM and Microsoft submitted proposals, but they were turned down. Instead, surprisingly, the government sought out the Christians of ICCC to provide the training. Why? "Capitalism does not work well without ethics," the Chinese government said. "You can provide our people with ethics in addition to the market economy training."

ICCC made sure the Chinese government understood that it is a Christian organization and that the course teaching would be based on the Bible. The government responded by saying, "You just can't say 'Jesus', 'God' or 'the Bible,'" but agreed it was acceptable to say, "It is written." The project moved forward, with Scripture quoted throughout the program ("A wise old saying says . . . " or "It is written . . . ").

The program has aired many times to a potential household audience of 250 million, and government leaders have documented more than 40,000 businesses that started as a result of the program. It is the only government-approved market economy course in the university system. Now, graduates of the course and owners of the businesses are asking, "Where do these wonderful sayings come from?"

Dale Neill, the international president of ICCC and coauthor and host on the series, can tell many extraordinary stories of how God is using this program to build a foundation within the nation of China that will surely have an enormous spiritual harvest in the years to come.

The series has now been translated into a number of other languages and is being used worldwide.

Flowers in Swaziland

Nan Jarvis is another example of someone who has been obedient to God in her workplace calling. She moved to Swaziland, a nation of one million people in the southern tip of Africa that leads the world in the number of HIV/AIDS cases, with more than 50 percent of the population infected. God had this farm girl from South Africa move to Swaziland to become a catalyst for transformation in this tiny nation.

Nan was born into a family of nine children, and her father committed suicide when she and her twin sister were just three and a half (her mother was pregnant at the time). She was sexually abused by her uncles, raped and physically abused by her own husband, and orphaned at the age of 24. Nan came to know Christ personally during this time, but after three years of marriage and then divorce, she and her son, Richard, moved to Swaziland.

Swaziland is a monarchy led by a king, and it is still heavily steeped in tribal ways. Nan owned a flower shop, and she just so happened to pick up the account for the king to deliver flowers to his five queens' households (later to be seven). As she was preparing the first flower arrangements, she felt that the Holy Spirit told her to make the deliveries herself. She wasn't too crazy about the idea as she had a person on staff to do this, but because she had an obedient heart, she did it anyway.

This act of obedience opened doors for her to get into people's homes, hospitals, clinics, schools, government offices, parliamentary houses and even into the king's palaces, where she has had many opportunities to be a witness, share the gospel, pray for people and see the hand of God touch and heal many lives. It is a difficult nation to work in because of deeply held tribal traditions, such as polygamy and sexual immorality, and erroneous foundations laid by their forefathers, such as ancestral worship and witchcraft.

Over time, Nan developed a relationship with many of the king's wives. One of these wives in particular eventually gave her life to the Lord and received the power of the Holy Spirit. This queen's life has radically changed over the years. She has implemented many things within her sphere of influence that have expressed her newfound faith. She earned a law degree and is now studying for her master's degree—which are things never achieved by a queen before—and has been admitted into the law court of the nation. She is promoting gospel music in the nation and has her own choir called "Redemption."

The king, queen mother and many of the other queens and leaders of the nation are professing Jesus Christ as Lord. Nan remains in a close relationship with the royal family, interceding by standing in the gap on their behalf as they bring about positive change to the nation. They are a nation under siege and undergoing a tremendous warfare for survival spiritually, socially and economically. The minister of Health and Social Welfare called for national prayer and time of repentance for the AIDS pandemic.

Nan's relationship with the people of Swaziland has opened doors for her to be a catalyst to bring agricultural programs into the nation through the ICCC and other groups. Jesus told her, "Go feed my sheep and care for my lambs." She has prayed and seen God send the rain that allowed people to eat once again. God has told her that Swaziland will become a "bread basket nation" and that it will feed itself and other nations. Nan is now in the medical profession, and sees God doing many mighty miracles in her daily marketplace. She is a wonderful example of how God can take a broken heart and heal it and use a person to impact a nation.

Making a Difference in Thailand

Ross Bridgman, an Australian, was attending a business seminar in Thailand when he decided to take a break and walk around the streets. As he walked, he noticed a young boy begging for food and was struck by the fact that he was allowed to be alone on the streets. The little boy took him to his mother, who proudly announced, "My son gets a meal every two days." Later, another woman approached him and offered to sell her two children for the equivalent of 25 dollars. Ross was deeply moved after seeing such desperate poverty. This, combined with a crisis that took place while he was in Thailand in which Ross almost lost his young daughter to an illness, made him rethink his priorities.

On his way back home to Australia, Ross was sitting in the airport when a man came over to introduce himself. Ross shared a little about the plight of the children in Thailand, and the man made a statement that he has never forgotten. "If you have a focus for people less fortunate than yourself, you will never go without a dollar." What made the statement even more profound was because of who it came from—Bill Gates, the founder of Microsoft.

When Ross returned home, he could not get the image of the children in Thailand out of his mind. He began to think about ways he could help them. At a seminar, he shared the dilemma of the Thai children with other business leaders and challenged them to consider the purpose for their lives. The attendees gave him $80,000 so he could return to Thailand and begin to change the conditions for these children.

During his return visit, Ross came up with a great idea to fund ongoing aid for orphans and to help people increase their business. Each day he left his hotel, he was approached by one or more *tuk-tuk* drivers (tuk-tuks are three-wheeled motorcycle taxis). There are about 1,000 tuk-tuks in Chiang Mai, a relatively small city, so competition was fierce. After a few days, he befriended one of the drivers who spoke some English and he learned about his business. Ross asked him if he would like to learn how to increase his revenue by incorporating some simple marketing strategies. The man said yes, so Ross explained that he would help this man at no charge if he would be willing to give 10 percent of the increase of his business to help fund the work with the orphans. The man readily agreed. Within a few weeks, his business increased fivefold, and he began contributing to the orphans. Today, that same model has been used to fund the care for over five hundred orphans in Thailand, India and China.

Hope for the City

Dennis and Megan Doyle are committed believers who own one of the largest commercial real estate companies in Minnesota. After noticing that many corporations had overstocks and overruns of merchandise and food that could be used to help the poor, they began to collaborate with corporations to get the excess goods for distribution through various ministries in the Minneapolis area, the nation and the world. The ministry, called Hope for the City, became so successful that in 2003 they gave away more than $100 million worth of goods. The ministry has given more than $300 million in the past three years.

Hope for the City partnered with four other Christian organizations to coordinate a large shipment of medical supplies to a communist country. They all met with the ambassador to the United Nations from the country, and after the meeting went to dinner and enjoyed each other's fellowship. It was obvious that the ambassador was touched by the sense of unity he felt among the Christian groups that were trying to help his country. Brenda Kilber of Hope for the City finishes the story:

Less than a week later, upon returning home, we received word that the ambassador had written our partner on the east coast and expressed to him that he had not seen before the kind of cooperation and friendship between organizations like he saw while he was with us. Having witnessed that kind of love and sharing, he was convinced that our faith in Jesus Christ was real and subsequently decided to put his trust in Jesus Christ as his personal Savior as well. He also said that he was going to make a strong recommendation to the leader of his country that they should allow Christians from America to come and help their people.

His cousin just happens to be the president of his country. This testimony is a powerful reminder to us. As we go about our daily work, we need to remember that the world is watching. More than what we say, the world is noticing what we do—in relationships with others, in partnerships in our everyday work life. When they see us interacting with each other, may they notice a love and a unity that can only come from Christ.

German Automaker in Ukraine

As a student in 1971, Berthold Becker was converted from being a socialist activist to a disciple of the Lord Jesus. Shortly after completing his university education, Berthold decided he wanted to understand what it meant to experience God in his professional career. So, until 1986, he learned to walk with God at work in the automotive industry. Berthold testifies how God gave him many designs for cars that became their bestsellers. He was often referred to as the "prophet" among his non-Christian auto executives.

With his wife, Barbara, as his personal intercessor, Berthold left his career in the auto industry to begin many entrepreneurial Kingdom initiatives. One was launched in the Ukraine through an initiative called GfS (*Gesellschaft für Strukturentwicklung*). Berthold became active in many training, consulting and joint venture situations, helping Ukrainian business start-ups. During his travels there, he noticed the lack of good bread, and he decided to do something about it. He started small businesses using mobile bakeries that he bought from the Swiss Army. The German and Ukranian governments soon recognized that Berthold had been serving the nation through his business expertise and came alongside him to say, "You are doing it better than we can." They started funding his enterprises, while his group remained in control of them.

Today, these enterprises (which include technology transfer and training centers for bread, meat and dairy products) have become a joint venture with a Ukrainian business group, operating successfully in the food industry.

Through stories like these, you can begin to see the new breed of Christian workplace leaders God is raising up today. Because we are all called to disciple the nations, God can use anyone to impact a nation. How might God want to use you in the days ahead? Are you willing to say yes to Him?

How About You?

1. In this chapter you learned that God is using workplace leaders to reach nations. Why do you think these people are able to be used by God in this way?
2. Name some ways your work might be used to make a difference in a nation.

THE POWER OF THE STAFF

It's 6:30 A.M., and CEO Jonathan Cooper is driving to work to meet with a management group in his technology company in San Marco, California. His six-year-old business is a leader in technology, with several award-winning products to its credit. It is known industry-wide for its quality products and superior customer service to its clients.

Jonathan is humming to himself as he drives. Although in many ways he looks like the other early-morning commuters rushing along the highway beside him, Jonathan is different. For one thing, on top of his briefcase on the seat next to him, improbably, there is a shepherd's staff. . . .

Yes, this staff is invisible to the casual observer, but Jonathan himself is aware of it as he drives to his office. Do you remember in chapter 1 how I described the significance of your staff? It is your God-empowered vocation, through which you can expect to influence your daily life in the working world. You don't have to be a CEO to make a difference with your staff. Every working person has one, including students, stay-at-home moms and those enlisted in the military. Are you an administrative assistant, a retail clerk or a government worker? Are you reading this book on your lunch break from your janitorial duties? Are you a corporate executive, a small business owner, an anesthesiologist or a dairy farmer? You get the idea. Let's return to Jonathan to see some "staffs at work"—not only his but also those of his employees.

Jonathan has already spent an hour and a half in prayer and Bible study in his home office. Arriving at the office after a 40-minute drive, he goes immediately to a room that has been designated as the worship and war room. Furnished with several comfortable chairs and couches as well as a conference table, the room is more like a living room than a boardroom. Here, every morning, employees gather for worship and prayer. Prayer topics range from personal concerns to new ideas that will help the business to requests for wisdom in operating the business from a godly perspective. The employees pray for customers and suppliers—and even for their competitors.

Jonathan calls his business a Kingdom business, and the 15 to 25 people who gather with him this morning agree. As he enters the room, music from the high-tech sound system greets him. Several others have already arrived and are on their knees in prayer or singing and worshiping God.

"Brothers and sisters," Jonathan begins, "please be in prayer for our new product development team who is seeking the Lord's direction for our new *PocketPhone*, a new half-dollar-size technology device that is designed to make people more mobile, allowing them to communicate hands-free. It clips onto your clothing and has a wireless microphone. If successful, it will replace the cell phone. The project manager got the idea for this project two months ago during our 6:30 A.M. prayer gathering. Some intercessors told us that they felt God was going to give the company a new innovative product that will transform the cellular phone industry."

It's now 8:00 A.M., and the company staff meeting is about to begin. Jonathan sits at the conference room table with the other members of his team. To his left is Jenny, a former IT director who now spends more time praying for the company than doing IT work. Jonathan recognized her gifting and insight during a time of difficult transition for the company. Often, she would come to him with thoughts she gained while interceding for the company. She had an extraordinary ability to confirm the decisions he was making, as it related to a particularly volatile time in the company.

Recognizing Jenny's value to the company, Jonathan created a new position for her: corporate intercessory director. Now, as the leader of a team of company intercessors, much of her time is spent praying for God's agenda for the company, for employees and clients, for other businesses in the city and for their city at large.

When asked about the unorthodox idea of having someone on staff who is paid to pray, Jonathan responded, "Funding the office of corporate intercessory director is the best investment I have ever made. The Lord has used Jenny to warn us of relationships that could have seriously derailed what we are doing. One time, we were involved in negotiations with a potential technology partner. Even though Jenny knew nothing about the negotiations, she was able to warn us that the company was not all that they portrayed themselves to be. We were able to close down negotiations and save time and money. I figure Jenny has saved our company hundreds of thousands of dollars over the last two years.

"Let me make this very clear: we do not use our intercessory team as seers. They are not crystal-ball gazers, but people who have a strong calling to prayer and a deep intimacy with the Lord that enables them to hear His voice clearly. However, it's not enough to have only them praying. I myself have a personal responsibility to intercede and seek God's direction on a daily—if not hourly—basis. Things work best when I'm faithful in that regard. I use the intercessor's reports to confirm the direction in which I've already sensed the Lord leading."

Now let's meet the rest of the management team. In addition to Jenny, there are seven people gathered around the table this morning; they are commonly known as the 411 Committee. Several years ago Jonathan's pastor taught on the five-fold ministry gifts found in Ephesians 4:11 and suggested that these gifts were applicable in the workplace as well as inside the local church. He encouraged Jonathan to put a leadership team in place that represented these five giftings. So, Jonathan began to identify those in his company who represented the office of apostle, prophet, pastor, teacher and evangelist.

Jonathan observed that as president, he modeled the traits of an apostle. At first that sounded weird to him. *Me, an apostle?* he thought. However, upon further study he learned that the word "apostle" simply means "sent one." Apostles often equate to entrepreneurs in the marketplace who have the vision and drive to start things. They lay new foundations just as the Early Church apostles did. He realized that was how he was wired; it was his spiritual DNA.

Jonathan could see the gift of a prophet operating in the company CFO, as he often forewarned the others about issues of which they should be mindful. The CFO had never thought of himself in these terms, but when Jonathan pointed out how he was already operating in the gifting, the CFO was encouraged to learn more about the role of the prophet. He learned that there were a number of variations of this gift, that there is an "office" of prophet and a "gift" of prophecy, and that the Bible says we are all encouraged to prophesy. As the CFO developed his understanding of this gifting, Jonathan saw how wonderfully it complemented his role at the company.

It did not take Jonathan long to realize that Bill, the company's sales director, probably had the gift of an evangelist. Bill often reported at meetings how the Lord had opened doors for him to have a conversation with someone about Christ. He had personally led more people to the Lord than anyone else in the company. It seemed to come so easy for him. In a way, it made sense: evangelist = salesman. So, whenever Jonathan does anything in the company that has an outreach focus to reach the lost, Bill is always front and center.

Janice is the company's marketing director. As Jonathan watched her operate, he realized that she probably had the gift of teacher. She is a great presenter of information and has an ability to cut right through to the core of the matter. She knows PowerPoint like the back of her hand. She makes the company look good in presentation meetings. She is detailed and does not like things to be out of order. She is a perfectionist to the *nth* degree. She leads a Bible study in the office and at her church. She also trains many of their employees about their corporate culture. People appreciate her professionalism. All these attributes of a teacher added up to "Jan." She could utilize her particular "staff" as she exercised her responsibilities for the marketing process in the company and for the corporate training.

Gerald is the human resources manager in the company. Following in the footsteps of his father, who was a successful engineer, Gerald had graduated from college with a degree in engineering. However, after a few years working as a mechanical engineer, his employer had fired him. Gerald had been like a ship without a sail when he met Jonathan at their church, and they became friends. Jonathan had listened to Gerald as he described working with many people from the church who were out of work. He seemed to have compassion for these people and was often a source of encouragement to them. Jonathan suggested that Gerald take a spiritual gifts test that was offered by his company's human resources department. Just as he thought, Gerald's results showed he was a pastor through and through. He began to talk with him about a career in human resources. Gerald loved people and loved helping them find their place. Now Gerald plugs people into the right place in the company and helps them become successful. He pastors the company and its employees in an ongoing way.

So, there you have it. The five-fold ministry is operating in Jonathan's high-tech company. He believes they have a solid spiritual foundation for all they are doing and he can attest that his company runs more smoothly than most churches he knows.

Jonathan credits his pastor and a local workplace ministry for helping him to understand and make these paradigm shifts in his work life. He receives a daily e-mail devotional made available through his church that encourages him and others to take their faith to the marketplace. They even have a church website with articles and resources for those in the workplace. He considers his pastor to be very progressive. In fact, he has never heard of any other church doing what his church does. They regularly have people share testimonies on Sunday about how God worked in their lives at their jobs that week. He has received training in his church on how to apply the Bible in specific workplace situations. He has also been asked to be on a focus group with the pastors to help the church leadership know how to break down the Word of God for application in work life situations. Often, their church has drama presentations that demonstrate ways to live out their faith at work. This church is involved in city transformation efforts and is part of a local coalition of churches.

Now back to the meeting. There are two others sitting around the table this morning. One is Jim, who works in the shipping department, but who also fulfills a much different role for the company.

Jonathan had attended a workplace conference not long ago in which a speaker urged business owners to get involved in city transformation, telling them that the pastors and churches could not achieve it alone without the broad-based involvement of the marketplace ministries. Jonathan began to pray about this and to take this exhortation to heart. Hearing that a group of pastors, marketplace ministries and intercessors were meeting on a regular basis for the purpose of transforming the city of San Marco, he decided to go and check it out.

Over time, as Jonathan sat quietly in the meetings and listened to the pastors' passion for their city, he began to get to know them. Occasionally, a need arose that Jonathan knew how to meet. It was not usually a financial need, but rather a technology issue that he knew how to solve for them. As time went on, this happened more and more. The pastors began to see Jonathan's contributions as more than just financial, and he became their friend and ally. Finally, the pastors embraced him because of his servant heart. For his part, Jonathan came to realize that pastors had a hard job and were often unappreciated, especially since they were expected to serve so many roles in their churches that they could not effectively lead at times.

As time went on, Jonathan became the marketplace representative in the group. He decided to allocate a portion of the profits from his company to the goal of city transformation—which is where Jim, the employee in his shipping department, comes in. Jonathan asked him to allocate a portion of his paid work time to this effort, and Jim became the transformation director for the company.

The big event that the company is planning at the moment is a city-wide prayer gathering. Jim is the point person. Jonathan's company decided to rent the stadium in the city in order to rally all of the churches and marketplace community around a day of prayer. In the process, pastors are beginning to become more unified with the marketplace ministries and business leaders in the city. It is becoming one of the most exciting things Jonathan has done through his company.

Finally, the last member of the 411 Committee sitting around the table this morning is Gwen, the director of Compassion for the City. Several years ago, Jonathan read in his Bible about how Jesus did not turn his head from the down-and-out of society, but had compassion for them and responded to their needs. Jonathan recognized that there was a big problem in San Marco. Many people were homeless in the city, and many others lacked the basic necessities of life.

At first, Jonathan assumed that other ministries were taking care of this need. But then he had an idea. He wondered what some of the major packaged-goods companies did with their excess or damaged goods. He made a few phone calls and found that some of the companies actually threw away some of these damaged goods. He could not believe this. He wanted to use these resources for the impoverished people of San Marco, so he decided to see if the companies would give their excess and damaged goods to him so that he could channel them to some of the downtown ministries.

Little did Jonathan know at the time that this would lead to the establishment of Compassion for the City. Now in its third year, Compassion for the City will distribute more than $100 million in goods through the urban ministries in their city. They have even sent goods overseas to Iraq and other needy parts of the world. Gwen, who is now the director of Compassion for the City, also happens to be one of the key intercessors in Jonathan's company.

It is now 6:00 P.M. and Jonathan is driving home from a full day of work. There was a time in his life when he seldom arrived home in time for dinner. His two kids never saw him. Rarely does he get home later than 6:30 P.M. now, which is certainly an improvement, as far as his family is concerned.

This represents a big change in Jonathan's life. He is a shaker-mover kind of guy who is motivated for success, but it almost cost him his family. A good friend challenged him one day by saying, "Jonathan, you are a great guy. You do so much for the community. You are successful. But you are blowing it with your family. If you continue down this path, you will wake up one day and have a rebellion in your household. Your kids will be seeking love in all the wrong places and your wife could leave you." His words cut Jonathan to the core. He realized that what his friend was saying was true. He saw how his wife and kids were becoming disconnected from him. He had been a committed Christian, but his business success had become too important to him.

Jonathan began to get help to discover the origin of his workaholism. He found that it was rooted in fear from the early days of his life when his father had died and the family insurance company failed to pay. His mother would often say that they did not have enough money for the needs of the family. Jonathan recalls saying to himself that he never wanted to experience that again. Jonathan decided to take a course at his church on generational strongholds. This led to freedom from this fear, and his work habits began to change.

Jonathan will tell you that his life is very different from what it used to be. His company is truly a Kingdom company. He does not know what the future holds, but he does know Who holds the future. He feels privileged to be a partner in business with the Lord Jesus.

This story is a realistic composite of the many lives profiled in this book. It gives us a glimpse into how we can experience the power of our staff when we experience Jesus' presence and power in and through all aspects of our lives—especially our work lives. God has called you to be in an intimate and exciting relationship with Him. He wants to use you to transform lives, workplaces, cities and nations.

Are you ready to begin?

BIBLE STUDY GUIDE

Part I: Understanding Your Call

Chapter 1
Satan's Deceptions About Your Work

1. In the first chapter, there is a story about John Wigington, who went to Bible school but felt he really wanted to be in business. Why do you think most people who are committed to Christ feel guilty being in business?

2. The chapter lists the following four deceptions that most people believe about ministry and calling:

    (1) Our jobs are not spiritual; they are useful only to make money for the church.
    (2) Our vocations have no spiritual authority.
    (3) Our secular employment is not to be mixed with the church's ministry activities.
    (4) "Ministry" is what takes place within the four walls of the church building.

    Describe the fruit of these lies and how they play out in Christians in the workplace today.

3. Read Genesis 3:17-19, which describes what was lost in the Garden when Adam and Eve sinned. Was work cursed as a result of the Fall? Describe the result of what happened to work when Adam and Eve sinned.

4. Read Luke 19:10 and Colossians 1:19-20. Describe what Jesus redeemed as a result of dying on the cross. Was it the salvation of men and women only?

5. Matthew 6:10 describes what Jesus wants to happen on Earth. Describe this prayer in your own words and what the world would look like if this prayer were answered.

6. In Matthew 21:1-3, Jesus requests the disciples to untie a donkey for Him to ride in Jerusalem. What does the donkey represent? How does that apply to you and me?

Chapter 2
Understanding Your Purpose

1. Read Ephesians 2:10. What is one reason why God created you?

2. Read Jeremiah 9:24 and Philippians 3:10, which both describe the primary reason why God created humans. What does this verse indicate to you?

3. A distinction is drawn in this chapter between a person's skill set and the purpose for which he or she is made. Based on these comments, how would you distinguish these two concepts?

4. Why is it important to know the purpose for which God made you?

5. A distinction is also made in this chapter between understanding your purpose and understanding your anointing. Explain the difference between these two concepts.

6. R. T. Kendall provides a good explanation of how a person becomes promoted outside their anointing. What happens when a person seeks to go outside of his or her God-given anointing?

7. Read 1 Corinthians 7:20. What do you think Paul is saying in this verse?

Chapter 3
Finding Your Purpose

1. Read Exodus 4:2-17. What does the staff represent in Moses' life? What was the first thing Moses had to do after God asked him, "What is that in your hand?" What is the implication for you and me?
2. Read 1 Samuel 9:6. What were some of the circumstances leading up to Saul being selected as the first king of Israel? Where were Moses and Saul when God came to them? What are some of the ways God comes to people in their work lives?
3. In his book *Experiencing God: Knowing and Doing His Will,* Henry Blackaby writes, "You cannot go with God and stay where you are." In other words, God must change you if you are to fulfill His purpose in your life. How do you think this plays out in the lives of Christians in the workplace?
4. Bob Mumford once said, "Beware of any Christian who does not walk with a limp." What do you think he means by that?
5. Name each of the four key tests that Joseph had to go through. Read Psalm 55:12-14. Which of the four key tests in the Joseph Process does this describe? According to this chapter, what is the only way to pass the test of purity?
6. Read John 10:11 and 12:25. What qualities of leadership are necessary to see God work in your work life?
7. Read Colossians 3:17,23-24. What will you receive if you are faithful to your work-life call?

Chapter 4
Four Attributes of an Effective Workplace Witness

1. Name the four attributes of a workplace witness that are cited in this chapter.
2. Read Daniel 1:19-20 and 6:1-3. What type of workers were Daniel and his friends?

3. Read Psalm 15. Describe the key characteristics of the person described in this psalm. What happens when a Christian fails to live an ethical life?

4. Someone once said, "People don't care how much you know as much as how much you care." Read Matthew 20:28. How does this comment relate to Jesus' words in that verse?

5. Read John 14:12. What does it mean to "do what Jesus did" in the context of your working life? Do miracles replace your work ethic? How would you define the importance of both concepts?

6. Could a non-Christian model all four of these characteristics? Why or why not?

Chapter 5
Four Types of Christians

1. Name four Christians who have had a significant impact on the world in the last 100 years. How many of these people that you listed were vocational ministry workers or workplace Christians?

2. Approximately 40 percent of the American population claims to be born again. Coca-Cola has a 40 percent market share in the soft drink industry. Do you think Christians have the same level of impact on the world as Coca-Cola has its on industry? Why or why not?

3. Ed Silvoso describes the following types of Christians in the workplace:

   (1) The Christian who is simply trying to survive.
   (2) The Christian who is living by Christian principles.
   (3) The Christian who is living by the power of the Holy Spirit.
   (4) The Christian who is transforming his or her workplace for Christ.

   Read Ecclesiastes 2:20,22-23. What type of Christian does this describe?

4. The second type of Christian is one who lives by Christian principles. Do you think this a good idea or a bad one? Describe why it may not be ideal.

5. Read 1 Corinthians 2:4-5. What distinction is Paul trying to make to the Corinthians?

6. What does God require from you in order to be one of those Christians who transforms his or her workplace for Christ? Describe some action steps that would be necessary to see your workplace transformed.

Chapter 6
The Religious Spirit and the Workplace

1. Dr. Peter Wagner defines a religious spirit as "an agent of Satan assigned to prevent change and maintain the status quo by using religious devices." Name some religious devices that might keep change from happening in a workplace situation.

2. Read 2 Corinthians 11:3. What do you think Paul is saying in this verse?

3. Read Galatians 3:1-5. What kind of human effort is Paul describing to the Galatians?

4. Name four examples of how the religious spirit shows up in the workplace.

5. Read 2 Corinthians 10:4-5. Spiritual strongholds seek to have you meet your primary needs through that stronghold. Describe how this happens.

6. Read Ephesians 3:16-18. What is Paul praying for in this passage? How might a spiritual stronghold keep you from experiencing this prayer?

Chapter 7
Bringing God to the 9 to 5 Window

1. For years, the organized church has focused their overseas mission efforts in reaching "The 10/40 Window," a region

where there are more unreached people groups than any-where else in the world. What would be the implications if God had a revival among those in the 9 to 5 Window?

2. A subscriber to the *TGIF* devotional states, "I never really considered my secular work as a ministry. . . . Now I feel I have as much a ministry as my pastor. I simply have a differ-ent mission field." What does this quote say about equality in calling? Does it lessen the vocational ministry worker or raise the non-vocational worker to a new spiritual level? Describe the distinctions between the two callings.

3. According to the evidence presented in this chapter, what is the reason a move of God has taken place in the public cor-porations of America?

4. George Barna says, "Workplace ministry will be one of the core future innovations in church ministry." How might this new focus change the way churches equip men and women for *their* calling in the workplace? What do you think will result from this new emphasis by the local church?

5. Dallas Willard states, "There is truly no division between sacred and secular except what we have created." Explain what you believe he means by this comment.

6. Dr. Wagner says, "I believe the workplace movement has the potential to impact society as much as the reformation did," which is a remarkable statement from a Church historian. Why do you believe this statement could be true? Or not true?

Part II: Bringing God's Power into Your Workplace

Chapter 8
Hearing the Voice of God—Even on the Job

1. Read John 10:14,27. Based on these verses, do you think that you can expect to hear and discern God's voice for yourself?

2. Read Acts 4:13, Luke 9:10 and Hosea 2:16,19-20. One of the keys to discerning God's voice is to know Jesus more intimately. What are some key points that you learn from these verses?

3. Read Revelation 21:2-9. What were some of the ways that Julian Watts and his company were intentional about coming into a new awareness that they were the Bride of Christ? What were some of the ways they were intentional about spending time in God's presence?

4. Read 1 Peter 1:8. What are some ways you can live out this verse daily?

5. List three things you can do to develop a more intimate relationship with Jesus personally and at work.

6. List the six ways God speaks throughout the Bible. Describe some ways God has spoken to you personally.

Chapter 9
Intercessory Prayer in the Workplace

1. Read Ephesians 6:18, Colossians 4:12, 1 Peter 2:5, Exodus 19:6 and Romans 8:26. Based on these verses, what does it mean to intercede in prayer?

2. Describe the three different levels of praying that are discussed in this chapter.

3. Cite some of the benefits the companies in this chapter have received from having paid intercessors on their staff. How has focusing on intercession been advantageous to these companies?

4. List three ways you could incorporate prayer in your workplace.

5. Describe each of the three ways, as explained in this chapter, that intercessors can be compensated in a business and the benefits or weaknesses of each.

6. Intercessors should not be used to direct your life, but rather to confirm what God has already spoken to you. What are some other cautions to be aware of when incorporating intercessory prayer in your workplace?

Chapter 10
Receiving Only What God Gives You

1. Read John 3:27. Describe the situation that prompted John the Baptist's response to his disciples' question. What does his answer indicate about his understanding of his purpose?
2. The story of F. B. Meyer, in which he encouraged his congregation to go to another church, is a wonderful of example of having a Kingdom perspective. What type of person would Meyer have had to be to do such a thing?
3. Read John 6:15. Jesus knew what He was to receive and when He was to receive it. How can you apply this same principle in your life?
4. Read Genesis 13:5-17. Why do you think Abraham might have been willing to give up his right as the elder and give Lot the choice land? What qualities are required in order to do this?
5. Read Ruth 1—3:15. Describe what took place when Ruth laid at Boaz's feet compared to when she went out to glean in the fields. What is a lesson you can learn from Ruth's example?
6. Read Numbers 20:9-11. Moses struck the rock out of anger, yet still achieved his goal of getting water from the rock. What is the danger in manipulating outcomes out of your own strength? What did Moses lose in the process?

Chapter 11
Do Not Reach for the Power

1. Read Psalm 33:16-17. Why does God warn against using your own skill and power?
2. Read Psalm 33:18-19 and Ephesians 6:10. What are some cautions given in these verses?
3. Read Judges 7:2-3. Why did God not want Gideon to have a larger army?

4. Read Joshua 6:1-21. Why did God prevent Joshua from using his army to defeat the people of Jericho?

5. Read Luke 14:28-30. What is the key warning being made in these verses?

6. There almost seems to be a paradox in Scripture on using your own natural skill versus placing total faith in God. Describe the principle of withholding your natural gifting to insure God is in it.

Chapter 12
Miracles at Work

1. Read Matthew 17:20. In the story of the miracle at Gunnar Olson's company, what were some of the steps that led him to stand against what took place? What is the difference between moving by the direction of the Holy Spirit or moving in presumption?

2. George Washington Carver was a great inventor. What did he cite as the key source of his inventions?

3. Among the several stories in this chapter, what were some common requirements for people to get their breakthrough miracles?

4. What is the difference between faith and risk?

5. What adjustments do you need to make to experience miracles in your work life?

6. Read Exodus 4:17. What are some miracles you would like to see happen through your "staff"?

Chapter 13
Transforming Your City

1. Read John 4:7-25,39. What did Jesus do that so impressed the woman at the well that she told her entire town about it?

2. Dr. Peter Wagner observed, "Not one U.S. city in America has been transformed." What reason did he give for that?

3. List the four requirements that Ed Silvoso cites are needed to see real transformation in cities.
4. What are the four other things listed in the chapter that are key to seeing transformation in cities?
5. Read 2 Chronicles 7:14 and Psalm 25:9. What are the key ingredients for the person God uses in transformation?
6. Read John 17:21. What is required for people to be able to respond to Jesus?

Chapter 14
From the Workplace to the Nations

1. Read Proverbs 22:29. What is the relationship between the person who is skilled in his or her work and a king?
2. What did Graham Power do after he had a vision from God? What often hinders most Christians from being used by God?
3. The story of Ross Bridgman relates how he solved a problem for other small businessmen and a problem in society. Describe the problem that motivated him to get involved.
4. The government of China solved a problem by seeking out the ICCC to provide training for its people in the new market-driven economy. Although ICCC had never done such a project, it was able to meet a need and impact a nation. What lessons can be learned from this example?
5. Berthold Becker created bakeries to serve the people in the Ukraine. Why did the Ukrainian government offer him money to create more bakeries? What lesson can you learn from this?
6. What are some ways you might use your work-life skills to benefit those who are less fortunate?

ENDNOTES

Chapter 1

1. Doug Sherman, *Discover the Word* radio program (Grand Rapids, MI: Discovery House Publishers, n.d.).

Chapter 2

1. R. T. Kendall, *The Anointing: Yesterday, Today and Tomorrow* (Nashville, TN: Thomas Nelson, Inc., 1999), p. 12. Italics in original.
2. Ibid., pp. 13-14.
3. Oswald Chambers, *Not Knowing Where: A Spiritual Journey Through the Book of Genesis* (Grand Rapids, MI: Discovery House Publishers, 1989), p. 45.

Chapter 3

1. *Vines Expository Dictionary of Old Testament Words*, P.C. Study Bible software (Nashville, TN: Thomas Nelson, 1985), commentary on Exodus 7:10.
2. Henry T. Blackaby, *Experiencing God: Knowing and Doing His Will* (Nashville, TN: Broadman and Holman Publishers, 1998), p. 132.
3. A. W. Tozer, *Root of the Righteousness* (Christian Publications, 1986), p. 137.
4. Henry T. Blackaby and Tom Blackaby, *The Man God Uses* (Nashville, TN: Broadman and Holman Publishers, 1999), n.p.

Chapter 4

1. Sheri Bell-Rehwoldt, "Why Like Ike?" *HR Innovator,* November-December 2004, p. 33.
2. Paul J. Meyer, *My Work Is My Ministry: They Are One and the Same!* (Waco, TX: Paul J. Meyer Resources, 2003), p. 18.
3. Gallup Organization and Princeton Religious Research Center, Secular Studies of Religious Behavior survey, December 1983.
4. Ram Charan and Jerry Useem, "Why Companies Fail," *Fortune*, May 2, 2002, p. 50.
5. Source unknown.

Chapter 5

1. "Annual Barna Group Survey Describes Changes in America's Religious Beliefs and Practices," The Barna Group, April 13, 2005. http://www.barna.org/FlexPage.aspx?Page=BarnaUpdateNarrow&BarnaUpdateID=186 (accessed April 2005).
2. Ed Silvoso, *Anointed for Business* (Ventura, CA: Regal Books, 2002), p.123.
3. Mike and Sue Dowgiewicz, *Restoring the Early Church* (Atlanta, GA: Aslan Group Publishing, 1996), p. 174. For a more complete examination of the Greek and Hebraic systems, see Mike and Sue Dowgiewicz, *The Prodigal Church* (pamphlet available through www.faithandworkresources.com).

4. Mark Markiewicz, "Business as Mission: How Two Grocers Changed the Course of a Nation," International Coalition of Workplace Ministries, August 16, 2001. http://www.icwm.net/articles_view.asp?articleid=8553&columnid= (accessed April 2005).

Chapter 6

1. C. Peter Wagner, *Freedom from the Religious Spirit* (Ventura, CA: Regal Books, 2005). p. 12. Italics in original.
2. Ibid., p. 14.
3. Frederick Nohl, *Luther* (St. Louis, MO: Concordia Publishing House, 1962), p. 26.
4. Mike and Sue Dowgiewicz, *Demolishing Strongholds* (Atlanta, GA: Aslan Group Publishing, 1996), p. 19.
5. Ibid.

Chapter 7

1. Parts of this chapter have been adapted from Os Hillman, "The Faith at Work Movement: Opening the 'Nine to Five' Window," *Regent Business Review.* http://www.regent.edu/acad/schbus/maz/busreview/issue9/faithatwork.html (accessed March 2005). Copyright 2003. Used by permission. All rights reserved.
2. Michelle Conlin, "Religion in the Workplace," *Business Week,* November 1999.
3. Marc Gunther, "God and Business," *Fortune,* July 2001, p. 59.
4. Russell Shorto, "With God at Our Desks," *New York Times Magazine*, October 31, 2004, p. 42.
5. Michael Ireland, "*Experiencing God* Author Sees Hope for Revival Among Businessmen." http://www.crosswalk.com/525158.html (accessed April 2005).
6. George Barna and Mark Hatch, *Boiling Point: Monitoring Cultural Shifts in the 21st Century* (Ventura, CA: Regal Books, 2001), p. 253.
7. Doug Sherman and William Hendricks, *Thank God It's Monday* radio program (Grand Rapids, MI: Discovery House Publishers, 2000).
8. Dallas Willard, *The Spirit of the Disciplines: Understanding How God Changes Lives* (San Francisco: HarperCollins Publishers, 1991), p. 214.
9. C. Peter Wagner, quoted in Os Hillman, *The Faith@Work Movement: What Every Pastor and Church Leader Should Know* (Atlanta, GA: Aslan Group Publishing, 2004), n.p.

Chapter 8

1. Ken Gire, *The Divine Embrace* (Wheaton, IL: Tyndale House Publishers, 2004), p. 24. Italics in original.
2. *Vines Expository Dictionary of Old Testament Words*, P.C. Study Bible software (Nashville, TN: Thomas Nelson, 1985), s.v. "propheteia."

Chapter 9

1. Darlene Maisano, *Breaking Open the Doors of Success Through Marketplace Intercession* (Santa Rosa, FL: Christian International Business Network, 2004), n.p.

Chapter 10

1. Steve Brown, *Key Life Ministries Radio Program* (Maitland, FL: 2003).
2. Oswald Chambers, *My Utmost for His Highest* (Grand Rapids, MI: Discovery House, 1989), n.p.

Chapter 11

1. Watchman Nee, *The Latent Power of the Soul* (Newspeak, NY: Christian Fellowship Publishers, 1972), p. 85.
2. Oswald Chambers, *Not Knowing Where: A Spiritual Journey Through the Book of Genesis* (Grand Rapids, MI: Discovery House Publishers, 1957), p. 122.

Chapter 12

1. John Woodbridge, ed., *More Than Conquerors* (Chicago: Moody, 1992), p. 312.
2. Ed Silvoso, *Anointed for Business* (Ventura, CA: Regal Books, 2002), p. 119.

Chapter 13

1. *Merriam-Webster's Dictionary*, s.v. "transformation."
2. Jackson Senyonga, "Revival the Hard Way," *Christianity Today.* http://www.christ ianitytoday.com/tc/2003/006/5.22.html (accessed April 2005).
3. C. Peter Wagner, quoted in Os Hillman, *The Faith@Work Movement: What Every Pastor and Church Leader Should Know* (Atlanta, GA: Aslan Group Publishing, 2004), foreword.
4. John Woodbridge, ed., *More than Conquerors: Portraits of Believers from All Walks of Life* (Chicago, IL: Mood Press, 1992), p. 337.
5. Ed Silvoso, *My City, God's City* (San Jose, CA: Harvest Evangelism, Inc., 2000), p. 7.
6. 2004 Year-End Report, Harvest Evangelism newsletter, p. 1.
7. Ed Silvoso, *Prayer Evangelism* (Ventura, CA: Regal Books, 2000), p. 208.

Additional Resources
by Os Hillman

FREE Email Devotional

Start your day by reading an email that encourages you to experience the Lord's presence at work. *TGIF Today God Is First* is a free daily email subscription which has a scripture verse and brief devotional applied to a workplace situation. Subscribe by going to: *www.marketplaceleaders.org*

Marketplace Mentor

Twice a month, receive more in-depth Biblical teaching on various topics related to your workplace calling, marketplace tips, proven business principles, and free and discounted resources via this email e-Zine. *When you subscribe you'll receive five free ebooks by Os Hillman.*

TGIF Today God Is First

365 Meditations on the Principles of Christ in the Workplace

The daily email devotional in book form! *Today God Is First* provides daily meditations that will help you focus your priority on knowing Jesus more intimately every day.
Hardback, 400 pp.

TGIF Paperback

180 devotionals presented by topics that range from God's will for your life to adversity. The smaller size and weight allows you to carry it with you wherever you go. Paperback, 286 pp.

TGIF Small Group Bible Study

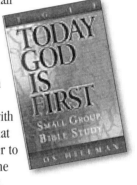

The popular *TGIF Today God Is First* book is now a 12-week, small group Bible study that is ideal for workplace groups. This study includes discussion questions; a workplace application with added scriptures that will allow the leader to extend or reduce the study time. Booklet, 48 pp.

Faith & Work: Do They Mix?

When you have an intimate relationship with Jesus, you will understand that your faith and work are not separate in God's eyes. This book will help you understand why your work IS your ministry. Paperback, 128 pp.

Making Godly Decisions

How can you know if you are making a decision that will be blessed by God? In *Making Godly Decisions*, you will learn the principles for making good decisions that are also godly decisions. Paperback, 80 pp.

The Purposes of Money

Why does God prosper some, while others still live in need? Can we trust God to provide when we don't have enough? In this book you will discover five fallacies of belief that most people live by regarding money. You will also learn the five primary reasons God gives us money. Paperback, 80 pp.

Called to the Workplace: *From Esau to Joseph*

One-day workshop, 6 audio tapes & workbook.

This is Os Hillman's complete one-day workshop that helps men and women discover their purpose in work and life. It is loaded with practical application principles to understand God's method of calling, biblical decision-making, and the role adversity plays in every believers life.

Are You a Biblical Worker?

Here's a self-assessment tool to help you discover where you are in your biblical knowledge of applying faith in your workplace. The inventory test features 50 True/False/Sometimes questions and answers. You will be challenged to think through workplace situations that most of us face every day. Also available as an online electronic test. Great for small group Bible studies.

The Faith@Work Movement

Is there a real move of God in the workplace? If so, what do pastors and church leaders need to know? How can the church mobilize workplace believers to impact their city and nation? *The Faith@Work Movement* by Os Hillman will answer these and many more questions about the modern-day faith at work movement. Foreword by Dr. Peter Wagner. Paperback, 128 pp.

Faith and Work Resources.com

Our resources site allows you to find the best in faith and work resources including books and CD messages. Plus you have access to programs such as the Affiliate Partnership which provides you with your own affiliate resource site - allowing you to earn income from your web site. *www.faithandworkresources.com*

Faith Makes a Difference
in the Workplace

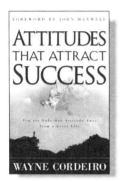

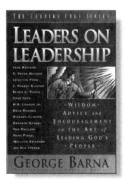

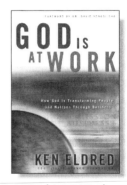